RUSS SHIP'

MUSIC
COURSE

A revolutionary new approach to understanding, reading & playing music

GUITAR

This book is dedicated to:

Chris Shipton – big brother who took
me by the scruff of the neck to buy
my first guitar

Ann & Bill Shipton – flexible parents
who never asked 'When are you going
to get a proper job?'

Acknowledgements

The author and publishers would like to acknowledge
the use of the following copyright material:

'Streets of London' by Ralph McTell (page 114)
© 1968 Westminster Music Limited,
19/20 Poland Street, London W1V 3DD.
International copyright secured.
All rights reserved. Used with permission.

'Wonderful Tonight', words and music: Eric Patrick Clapton (page 116)
© 1976 Throat Music Limited
Reproduced by kind permission of Chappell Music Limited,
129 Park Street, London W1Y 3FA.

'Sultans of Swing' by Mark Knopfler (page 118)
© 1978 Straitjacket Songs Limited
Reproduced by permission of Rondor Music (London) Ltd,
10a Parsons Green, London SW6 4TW.

'Nights in White Satin' by Justin Hayward (page 120)
© 1967 Tyler Music Limited,
19/20 Poland Street, London W1V 3DD.
International copyright secured.
All rights reserved. Used by permission.

First published 1988 by Pan Books Ltd,
Cavaye Place, London SW10 9PG
9 8 7 6 5 4 3 2 1
© Russ Shipton 1988
ISBN 0330 30403 8
Photoset by Parker Typesetting Service, Leicester
Music by Halstan & Co. Ltd, Amersham
Printed and bound in Spain by
Mateu Cromo S.A., Madrid

CONTENTS

THE BASICS OF THE MUSIC SYSTEM

- 8 Sounds and pitch
- 10 Vibrations and notes
- 12 Octave notes
- 14 Semitones
- 16 Naming notes
- 18 The repeating octave system

THE KEY SYSTEM

- 20 Melody and the tonal centre
- 22 Expected notes
- 24 The general major scale
  The C major scale
- 26 Other major scales
- 28 Harmony
- 30 Chordal accompaniment
- 32 Minor chords
- 34 Extended chords – 7ths
- 36 Minor keys
- 38 Summary of the key system

THE VISUAL MUSIC SYSTEM – PITCH

- 40 The stave
  Notes on the treble clef
- 42 Leger lines
  Sharp or flat notes
- 44 Key signatures
  Accidentals
- 46 The bass clef

THE VISUAL MUSIC SYSTEM – RHYTHM

- 48 Beats and bars
- 50 Rhythm patterns 3- and 4-beat
- 52 Note lengths
- 54 Time signatures – $^4_4$
- 56 The $^3_4$ time signature
- 58 Rests
- 60 8th note rests in $^4_4$ and $^3_4$
- 62 Ties within a bar
- 64 Ties across bar lines
- 66 Dotted half- and quarter-notes
- 68 Sixteenth-notes
- 70 Tied sixteenth-notes
  The sixteenth-note rest
  The dotted eighth-note
- 72 Summary of notes and rests in $^4_4$ and $^3_4$
  Note spacing in sheet music

- 74 The $\mathcal{C}$ time signature
- 76 The $^2_4$ time signature
- 78 The $^3_8$ time signature
- 80 The $^6_8$ time signature
- 82 The $^{12}_8$ time signature
- 84 The eight-note triplet
  The quarter-note triplet
- 86 The swing rhythm
  Triplets

GUITAR MUSIC NOTATION

- 88 Standard and two-part notation
- 90 Fingering and interpretation signs and terms
- 92 Tablature notation
- 94 Standard and tablature notation together
  Guitar embellishments and signs

WORKING OUT AND TRANSCRIBING MUSIC

- 96 Working out music
  Transcribing music

ARRANGING FOR THE GUITAR

- 100 Solo guitar accompaniment
- 101 The arpeggio style
- 102 The alternating thumb style
- 103 The monotonic bass style
  The slap style
- 104 The bass-strum style
- 105 The strumming style
- 106 Arranging for rhythm guitar in a band
- 108 Arranging for lead guitar in a band
- 110 Arranging for instrumental solo guitar
- 112 Arranging for two or more guitars

SHEET MUSIC EXAMPLES

- 114 Streets of London
- 116 Wonderful Tonight
- 118 Sultans of Swing
- 120 Nights in White Satin

APPENDICES

- 122 Appendix 1 – Pitch
- 126 Appendix 2 – Rhythm
- 127 Appendix 3 – Interpretation
- 128 A note from the author

INTRODUCTION

General

A great deal of mystique surrounds the subject of music theory among many musicians – professionals as well as amateurs and beginners. Perhaps it has acquired an aura of complexity it doesn't deserve because books about reading music concentrate on presenting the mechanics of the system, complete with jargon, and encourage the student to learn the material 'parrot fashion'. At some point in the future, he or she is expected to realize how and why the various component parts fit together.

This book has been written with the assumption that the reader has no musical knowledge whatsoever. It takes him or her step by step through each point of music theory with clear and straightforward explanations. Those of you who do have some grasp of music theory and notation, but don't fully understand how the music system works, should still go through the book from start to finish, because each piece of music theory is placed in logical order and related to what has been explained previously.

Sections and layout

All the theory in the book is illustrated by examples for you to play, and the layout will make it easier for you to follow and learn the material. Each double-page spread covers one point of music theory only – the left-hand page gives you the theory, and the right has examples for you to practise.

The first section gently introduces the basics of the music system – sounds and pitch, how notes are named, and the repeating octave system. The second section deals with the concept of key – the relationship between melody, scales and chords is examined thoroughly. The third section then looks at standard music notation for the pitch of notes, and how the key system is represented in written music. The fourth section deals with the nature of rhythm and its underlying stress patterns – represented by beats and bars. It explains how the length of notes and rests is written, and shows the student how to follow and play music while counting the beats.

The fifth section shows how music written specifically for the guitar is presented in tuition manuals and songbooks, the sixth deals with working out and transcribing music and the seventh discusses the broad subject of arranging for the guitar in all its various guises. Examples from the actual sheet music of popular songs are given in the last section of the book*, with a full analysis for you to see how the information in the first seven sections can be put to use.

* apart from the appendices – these include a brief explanation of other facts and terms that you may come across and need to understand.

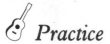

Music should be heard as well as read, so this theory book (unlike others) gives due emphasis to the practical side. Apart from making the task of learning to understand and read music much easier, it is essential to hear and 'feel' the relationship of notes by playing them on your chosen instrument. Intervals, chords and rhythm patterns can only be fully understood by playing and hearing them. Each and every point of music theory in the book is backed up with one or more practical examples to play on your guitar.

Today's written music

You'll come across written music (in standard notation or tablature) in sheet music, songbooks and instruction manuals, and will need to read and follow it, play it on the guitar, and re-arrange it to suit you, your musical instrument and your musical taste – this book provides the information for you to learn how to do all these things.

Transcribing recorded music

You may have music on tape, records or video, but no transcription of it in sheet music or songbooks; or you may want to write down your own songs and instrumentals. In addition to the information in the main sections, towards the end of the book I've included useful hints and guidance for you to work out and transcribe music yourself.

Matching cassette

A matching cassette has been produced for this book. It includes demonstrations on the guitar of all the music examples from every section of the book – so you can check that what you're playing is correct.

THE BASICS OF THE MUSIC SYSTEM

Sounds and pitch

A sound is a movement of the air that the ear registers – a door closing, someone speaking, the lapping of waves on the seashore. These actions all result in sounds that our ears can hear.

Some sounds are recognized as being higher than others. The scrape of a knife is higher than the rumble of a lorry engine: the small dog's bark is shriller than the large dog's. The height or depth of sounds is called 'pitch'.

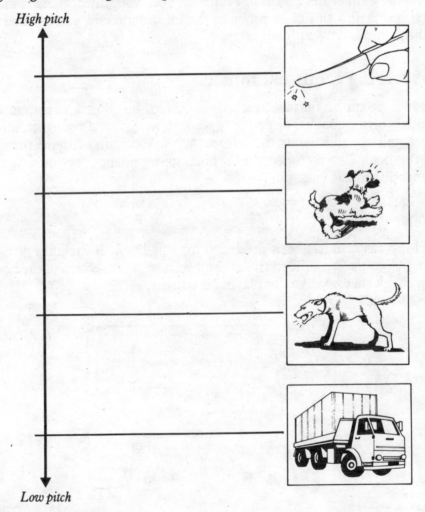

Not all sounds are notes, of course. Before a sound can be called a note, it must have a constant level of air vibration.

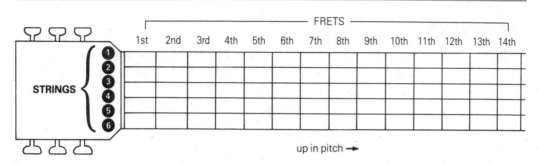

The diagram above shows the guitar fretboard roughly as you see yours when holding the guitar and looking down across the strings.

Open string notes

Strike the open 1st string with a flatpick or right-hand finger ('open' means when there is no left hand finger pressing down on it). The 1st string is the one nearest the floor when holding and playing the guitar, indicated ❶ on the diagram above. It is the thinnest string and higher in pitch than all the other strings. Now play the open 6th string, the thickest, and lower in pitch than all the others. The strings between these outside two are pitched progressively lower as you go towards the 6th string – the 2nd string is a little lower in pitch than the 1st string, the 3rd lower than the 2nd string, and so on. Play all the strings one after the other from high pitch to low pitch and back.

Fretted notes

A fretted note is produced when a left-hand finger presses down on the fretboard. Using the fingertip of your first or second left-hand finger, press down the 6th string at the 1st fret (indicated in the diagram above). Press down on the string just behind or to the left of the fretwire, and then strike the string. You'll notice that the pitch of the 1st fret note is higher than the pitch of the open string note. As you move towards the body of the guitar, you'll hear the fretted notes on each of the strings rising in pitch.

Vibrations and notes

When the air is vibrated more quickly, the resulting sound will be higher in pitch. If the vibrations are not so frequent, the sound will be lower in pitch.

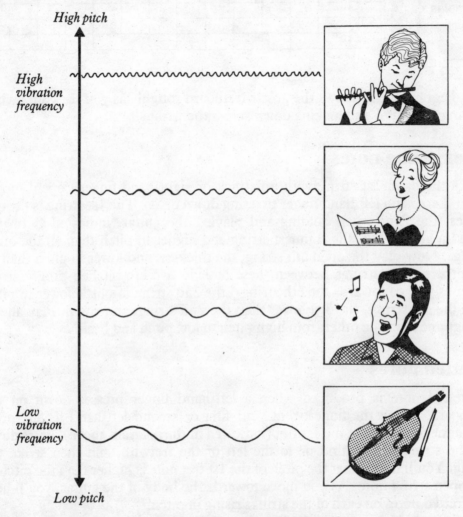

When a sound is held at the same recognizable level of pitch, it means that the vibrations are staying at the same frequency. When this happens, the sound can be given a name to indicate the particular level of pitch.

When a sound has a constant level of vibration and can be easily measured for pitch, it can be called a note. Normally sounds are said to be notes only when they are produced by voices or musical instruments.

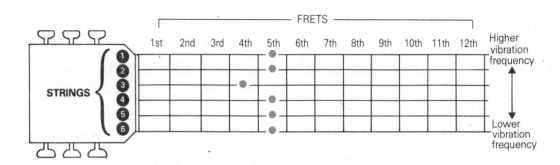

String vibrations

Strike the 1st string on your guitar. The vibrating string causes the air to vibrate and the soundbox of the guitar amplifies the volume of the resulting sound (in the case of the electric guitar, the pick-ups convert the vibrations into electric impulses and the amplifier and speakers convert them into sound). Because the string vibrates the air at a constant rate, a note is produced that remains the same pitch as long as the string continues to vibrate.

The thinner strings are designed and tuned to vibrate more quickly and produce higher pitched notes, while the thicker strings are made and tuned to vibrate more slowly for lower notes.

Tuning your guitar

Guitar strings are normally tuned to what is known as 'standard tuning'. If you have the matching cassette for this book, listen to the pitch of my guitar strings at the beginning and tune your strings directly to each of them. Otherwise, obtain an 'A' tuning fork and follow the usual tuning procedure.

(*a*) Tap one prong of the tuning fork on your knee and then hold the single end on the guitar body. The fork vibrates at a constant rate, producing a note that should be the same as the 1st string stopped at the 5th fret – as indicated by the dot on the diagram above. Adjust the string up or down until the 5th fret of the 1st string is the same pitch as the tuning fork.

(*b*) Now you can tune your other strings to the 1st string, going from treble (higher pitch) to bass (lower pitch). The diagram above shows the fret positions to press. The 5th fret of the 2nd string should be the same note as the open 1st string, so play the two notes and tighten or loosen the 2nd string until it's the correct pitch. The 4th fret of the 3rd string should be the same pitch as the open 2nd string, so adjust it till the two notes are the same. Then the 5th fret of the other strings should be the same pitch as the higher open string note, i.e. 5th fret 4th string = open 3rd string, 5th fret 5th string = open 4th string, 5th fret 6th string = open 5th string.

Octave notes

The pitch of notes can vary from an extremely low level to an extremely high level. If we gave a different name to each note there would be too many to deal with. To produce a manageable music system, some way of breaking up the huge range of pitch is necessary.

The first of two ways to divide up the range of possible notes is the naming and use of 'octave notes'. Two notes of exactly the same pitch are called 'unison notes', and when we hear unison notes our ears can tell quite easily that they are at the same level of pitch. Though octave notes are reasonably far apart in pitch, we can quickly recognize them too.

Every note has octave notes above and below it in pitch, and they all have a scientifically measurable relationship to one another – pitch can be measured by the number of vibrations per second produced by a note, and one octave note has twice as many vibrations per second as the octave note below it.

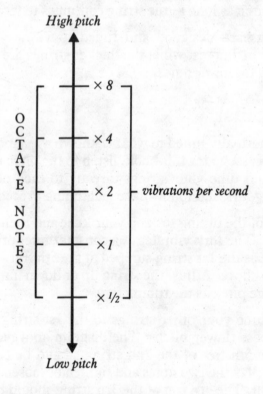

Because octave notes are easy for the ear to recognize, and are considered so 'similar' to each other, we give them the same name – and therefore the range of pitch is divided into sections known as 'octaves'.

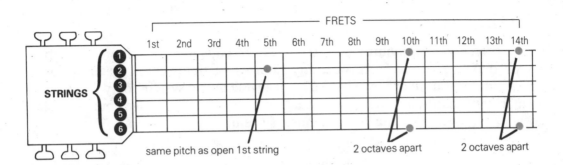

Unison notes

Play the open 1st string, followed by the note at the 5th fret of the 2nd string. These two notes should be exactly the same pitch, i.e. unison notes, as you'll remember from the tuning procedure you went through earlier. Though the 'timbre' or tone quality of the two notes may be a little different (because one note is produced by an open string and the other is a fretted note, and because the strings are of different thicknesses), the pitch is the same. With a little practice and time you'll be able to recognize unison notes, wherever they're played on the fretboard.

Octave notes

Now play the open 6th string followed by the note at the 2nd fret of the 4th string, and finally the open 1st string. Do you recognize the strong similarities between these three notes? Well, they are octaves of each other – the open 1st string note is two octaves above the open 6th string, and the 2nd fret of the 4th string is the octave note between them. All three notes are therefore given the same name.

Because the open 1st and open 6th string have the same name, it follows that notes at the same fret on each of the two strings always have the same name too – the notes are always two octaves apart. See if you can find other octave notes in different places on your guitar fretboard.

Semitones

The second way of dividing up the range of pitch is to have a minimum gap in pitch between notes. In theory, any number of notes could occur between octave notes, but in order to have a manageable music system, only those notes which have 'naturally harmonious relationships' with the octave notes and each other are now used in the western music system.

Today, the smallest interval in pitch between one note and another is called a 'semitone', and the distance in pitch between any note and the next of the same name (i.e. between octave notes) is twelve semitones.

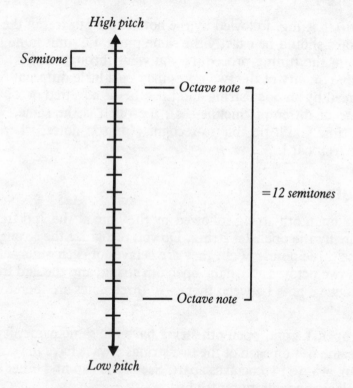

The diagram above shows that there are just twelve notes in an octave, or in other words the distance in pitch betwen two notes of the same name an octave apart is always twelve semitones.

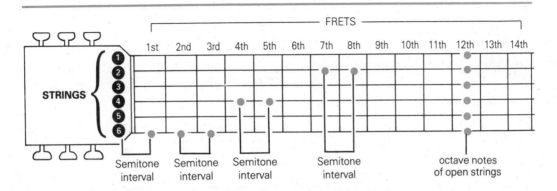

One fret = one semitone

As indicated in the diagram above, any two notes on adjacent frets are a semitone in pitch apart – including an open string note to a 1st fret note. Play the two notes next to each other on the 2nd and 3rd frets of the 6th string, for example. There is a semitone interval between them. Now play the open 6th string, then the 1st fret note – again they are a semitone apart. Though the fretwires gradually come closer together as you move up the fretboard towards the guitar body, fretnotes next to each other are always a semitone apart in pitch. Play the 7th and then 8th fret on the 2nd string, for example, and hear the same semitone interval.

The guitar fretboard, set up with notes at semitone intervals, is similar to many other instruments. The piano and other keyboard instruments have keys that are a semitone apart, and woodwind and brass instruments can also move up and down in pitch semitone by semitone. The different instruments vary mainly in tonal quality and in the range of pitch they can cover.

Octaves on the guitar

Play all the notes on the 1st string from the open string to the 12th fret. You should notice the similarity between the open string and 12th fret notes – they're octave notes. There are twelve semitones between one octave note and the next, so the octave note for each open string can be found at the 12th fret of the same string. Play the open 2nd string followed by the 12th fret of the 2nd string, then the open 3rd string followed by the 12th fret of the 3rd string, and so on. If your guitar is well made, each pair of notes should be 'perfect' octaves of each other.

Naming notes

In Europe, since well before the Middle Ages, letters of the alphabet have been used as names of notes. The scale and key system in operation today involves the use of the first seven letters of the alphabet.

⟶ *up in pitch*

A   B   C   D   E   F   G   A   B   C

Going through the letters in alphabetical order means getting higher in pitch. When **G** has been reached, another **A** comes round and the seven letters occur again. The same letter that occurs again is an octave higher than the previous one – so the second **A** shown above is an octave higher than the first **A**; the second **B** is an octave higher than the first **B**, and so on.

Sharp and flat notes

There are 12 semitones/notes in one octave, but only seven letters of the alphabet are used – leaving five semitone notes still to be named. Sometimes these notes are named using a sharp sign (♯), and sometimes they are named with a flat sign (♭). Here are all 12 semitone notes in one octave, starting with the **A** note:

├──────── *One Octave = 12 Semitones* ────────┤

A   A♯   B   C   C♯   D   D♯   E   F   F♯   G   G♯   A
    [B♭]   **[D♭]**   **[E♭]**   **[G♭]**   **[A♭]**

You'll notice that there is no intermediate note between **B** and **C**, or between **E** and **F**. In other words they are just one semitone apart. Between all the other notes there is an intermediate note, sometimes called a sharp, sometimes a flat note, i.e. **A♯** may be called **B♭** depending on the context, **C♯** may be called **D♭**, **D♯** may be called **E♭**, and so on. You can think of these intermediate notes as the letter below plus a semitone (**A♯** for example) or the letter above minus a semitone (**B♭** for example).

On the piano keyboard, there are two places in each octave where white keys lie next to each other with no black key between – this is where the notes **B** and **C** and **E** and **F** occur.

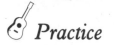
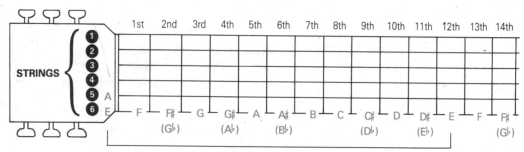

One octave = 12 semitones/frets

Notes on the 6th string

Play the open 6th string – in standard tuning this is an **E** note, the lowest note on the guitar fretboard. Now play the note at the 1st fret. This is one semitone higher in pitch than the open string, and because there is no intermediate note between **E** and **F**, it must be an **F** note. The 2nd fret on the 6th string is a semitone higher than the 1st fret **F**, so it must be an **F♯** or **G♭**. The 3rd fret is a **G** note, the 4th fret a **G♯** or **A♭**, and so on till the **E** note at the 12th fret – which you'll remember is an octave higher than the open string **E** note. From the 12th fret, the notes repeat, so the 13th fret is an **F** note, an octave higher than the 1st fret **F**, the 14th fret an **F♯** or **G♭**, and so on.

Notes on the 5th string

The 5th string in standard tuning is an **A** note – this is five semitones higher in pitch than the open 6th string **E** note. That's why the same **A** note can be found at the 5th fret of the 6th string. When moving up the frets of the 5th string, the notes will go along the alphabet, with intermediate sharp (or flat) notes, in the same way. So the 1st fret of the 5th string will be an **A♯** or **B♭**, the 2nd fret will be a **B** note, the 3rd fret a **C**, and so on. Play each of the notes on the 5th string, then write them on the diagram above.

Remember that a note on the 5th string can also be found on the 6th string, five frets further along towards the body of the guitar. These pairs of notes are the same pitch, i.e. unison notes, not octaves of each other.

The repeating octave system

You've seen that notes an octave apart in pitch are considered similar enough to be given the same name, and that the smallest interval of pitch to be given a name is a semitone. Octave notes and semitones provide us with a manageable system of 'repeating octaves' of twelve notes or semitones.

You've seen that only the first seven letters of the alphabet are used to name notes, plus sharp (♯) or flat (♭) signs for the remaining five notes in each octave. Here is a summary of what you've learnt so far:

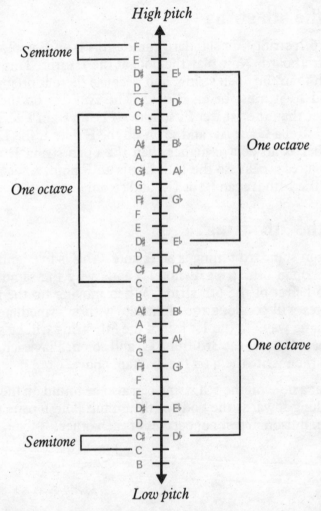

In the repeating octave system, one octave and its twelve semitones and notes is essentially the 'same' as any other. The octave from an **A** to the next **A** is basically the same as the octave from an **E♭** to the next **E♭** – both cover an octave in pitch and include exactly the same twelve semitones and notes, albeit in a different sequence.

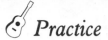

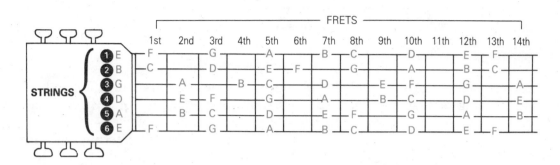

The guitar fretboard

On the previous practice page you named and played the notes on the 5th and 6th strings – because most chords have their root notes on these strings (examined later) it is worth trying to memorize some of them. It is also worth trying to remember other notes on the fretboard – to begin with you could try to commit the first five frets to memory, and then you'll be able to pick out most melodies quickly.

Notes on the higher frets of the fretboard can be worked out easily by working back from the octave notes at the 12th fret. The essential things to remember are the open string notes, and the fact that there is a sharp or flat note between every letter except **B** and **C** and **E** and **F**. Knowing these two things will enable you to work out any note on the fretboard.

No sharp or flat notes are shown in the diagram above. Play and fill in the intermediate notes.

Unison notes

You saw that notes of the same pitch can be found on the 5th and 6th strings. In fact unison notes can be found all over the fretboard – the same note can be found five frets higher on the next string (the one lower in pitch, of course), with the exception of the 2nd string notes. These are found just four frets further along on the 3rd string. Guitarists use different unison notes because it makes fingering easier, or for a particular tonal quality that the string produces. Try finding unison notes yourself, and listen to the differences in timbre or tonal quality of each string.

THE KEY SYSTEM

Melody

The essence of music is melody. Melody is a series of consecutive notes that can be sung or played. When our ears hear a melody, they quickly register (consciously or subconsciously) the note round which it revolves – the tonic note. This is the most important or fundamental note, and it determines what is called the 'key' of the music.

The tonal centre

The tonic note represents the tonal centre of a piece of music. As we listen, we become aware of the tonal centre and expect the melody to return to it. Tension is created by moving away from the tonal centre, and the anticipated resolution occurs when the music finally comes to rest on the tonic note.

To help you understand the idea of a tonal centre and key for a piece of music, here is a simple and well-known melody presented in graph form. The pitch of the notes is shown vertically and the approximate duration on the horizontal. The individual notes have been joined together to form a continuous line.

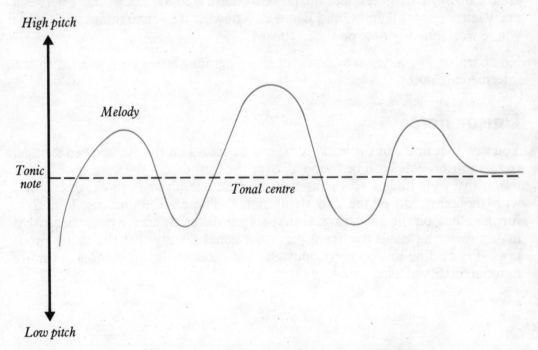

The tonal centre is shown as a dotted line, and the melody ends on the tonic note. The 'doh', in the doh, ray, me, fah, soh, lah, te, doh series that we all learn when young, represents the tonic note – as you'll see shortly.

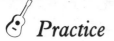

Listening for the tonal centre

Play the following notes in the order given (don't worry about the timing or length of notes). The string number is given first, with the fret position below.

String	3	2	2	1	2	2	1	2	2	3	3
Fret	0	1	1	0	3	1	0	3	1	2	0

This is just the first line of the sample melody shown on the previous page in graph form. Play the notes through a couple of times, and see if you can guess what the tonic note (tonal centre) is. Imagine the tune coming to an end – which note do you feel would provide a strong or complete resolution to the music?*

Recorded music

To help you understand the idea of music having a tonal centre, listen to songs and instrumentals that you know, and try to work out the tonic note that the melody is 'revolving around' and you expect it to end on. Listen to the music for a while and then sing or 'la' the tonic note as soon as you think you know it. Then listen to the last note of the song (or each chorus) and see if you guessed right. Now do the same thing with songs or music you're not familiar with (i.e. on the radio). It's important for you to get the 'feel' of tonal centres, as they are the basis of the key system used for all western music.

Matching cassette

On the matching cassette I've played the sample melody notes given above, plus two other short sequences for you to listen to and work out the tonic notes involved.

* 1st fret, 2nd string.

Expected notes

Once the tonal centre of a piece of music has been established, the key is also fixed. The key tells us what notes are expected (by our conditioned western ears!) when a certain note is the tonic note. These expected notes have particular harmonic relationships with the tonic note and each other – relationships that feel right, and are now accepted as normal in western music.

Doh ray me fah soh lah te doh

The basis of the key system today is the 'doh ray me fah soh lah te doh' sequence. Learning this sequence of notes fixes these particular tonal relationships in our mind. The doh is the tonic note, and each of the other notes is a specific distance in pitch from it. They hold set positions in the series, leading to the next doh, which is one octave higher. With doh as the tonic note, the expected notes in a melody will be drawn from this series. These notes produce an 'acceptable' level of tension, which is then resolved to the listener's satisfaction when the melody ends with the tonic note. Using the doh ray me series, the simple melody you've just seen in graph form could be shown like this:

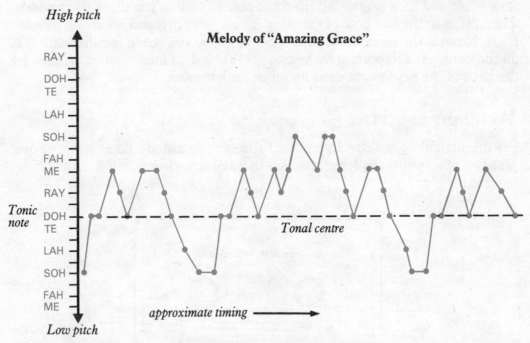

The level of pitch is marked off with the doh ray me fah soh lah te doh notes, and a dot given for each melody note. Though the melody ends on the doh or tonic note in the 'middle' of the melody line, it could end on the higher or lower doh. Also the other notes from the series can be drawn from higher or lower octaves.

FRETS

	1st	2nd	3rd	4th	5th	6th	7th	8th	9th	10th	11th	12th	13th	14th

SOH (open string) LAH TE DOH (tonic) RAY ME FAH SOH LAH

'Amazing Grace'

You've seen the melody of 'Amazing Grace' in graph form, which should have given you a general idea of the 'shape' of a melody and how it relates to the tonal centre or tonic note. Here are the words and the notes for each syllable (some syllables involve more than one note):

Line 1 **soh doh doh me ray doh me me ray doh lah soh**
A ——— maz—ing ————— grace, how —— sweet the sound

Line 2 **soh doh doh me ray doh me ray me soh**
That —— saved a ————— wretch like —— me

Line 3 **me soh soh me ray do me me ray doh lah soh**
I ——— once was ———— lost, but —— now am found

Line 4 **soh doh doh me ray doh me ray doh**
Was —— blind, but ———— now I see.

You can play the whole melody of 'Amazing Grace' on one string – in fact on *any* string. As long as the relationship of the notes remains the same, music can be played at different levels of pitch with different tonic notes. Play the melody on each string in turn, beginning with the 6th. For the first note, soh, play the open string. The doh is then found at the 5th fret of the string. All the notes are indicated on the diagram above – notice that te and doh, and me and fah are just one fret or semitone apart, while the other notes are two frets apart. This matches the note spacing on the melody graph opposite.

Matching cassette

'Amazing Grace' is played at different levels of pitch on the matching cassette. These levels of pitch are called keys, and the expected notes in a particular key are indicated by a scale or series of notes going from the tonic note to the note of the same name an octave higher. The doh ray me fah soh lah te doh series is a *general* scale, i.e. one that applies to any level of pitch.

The general major scale

A scale is a series of notes going from one note to the next note of the same name, and the doh ray me fah soh lah te doh sequence is one of many possible scales. Over the last three centuries, this particular scale has established itself as the basis for western music – it is called 'the major scale'.

The doh ray me fah soh lah te doh series can be called a 'general' major scale, because the doh (i.e. the tonic note) isn't fixed at a particular pitch. The intervals between each of the notes, however, always remain the same, so whatever the level of pitch chosen the notes will produce a major scale. These intervals of pitch between the notes of a major scale are: tone, tone, semitone, tone, tone, tone, semitone. (The tone is, as you'd expect, equivalent to two semitones.)

Now you'll appreciate why there was a smaller gap in pitch between me and fah and te and doh on the previous melody graph – the scale is made up of notes with both tone and semitone intervals between them.

The C major scale

When the doh ray me fah soh lah te doh major scale is 'fixed' at a particular level of pitch, it will be given the name of the tonic note, i.e. if the note the scale begins and ends on is the **C** note, then the scale will be called the '**C** major scale'.

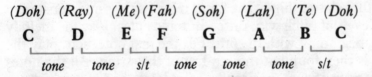

You'll notice that the **C** major scale has no sharp or flat notes – this is because **E** and **F** and **B** and **C** are only a semitone apart, and these notes fall in the semitone positions of the **C** major scale. Therefore, when a song is written in 'the key of **C** major' (i.e. with **C** as the tonic note), the notes that are expected to be used will be drawn from the scale of **C** major – **C D E F G A B C**.

Follow the notes indicated on the guitar fretboard below and play the **C** major scale – firstly on the 2nd string, beginning with the 1st fret **C** note and ending with the 13th fret **C** note an octave higher; then play the **C** major scale an octave lower, starting with the 3rd fret of the 5th string and ending on the 15th fret.

Notice the semitone (= one fret) and tone (= two frets) intervals between the notes. As you saw on the previous page, the **C** major scale includes no sharp or flat notes because the **B** and **C** notes and the **E** and **F** notes happen to fall in the 'semitone positions' of the major scale when **C** is the tonic note.

Playing across the strings

When guitarists play scales, they usually go *across* the strings rather than along the same string – there is much less movement for the left hand. Play the **C** major scale shown below, which includes the open 4th, 3rd and 2nd string notes, using your left-hand index finger for the 1st fret notes, the middle finger for the 2nd fret notes, and ring finger for the 3rd fret notes.

When you play the notes of the **C** major scale, remember that the **C** note is the tonic note – the most important note. The **C** major scale provides the notes for music written in 'the key of C major'. So when a piece of music or a song is written in 'the key of C' (for short), the tonic note and tonal centre is **C** and the expected melody notes will be: **C D E F G A** and **B**. These notes can come from more than one octave.

Other major scales

Major scales other than **C** will involve one or more flat or sharp notes. Write down seven different letters, plus the tonic note to finish, then adjust them up or down with a sharp or flat sign to produce the correct major scale intervals, i.e. tone, tone, semitone, tone, tone, tone, semitone. Let's take the **G** major scale, for example. The tonic note is **G** and the scale therefore begins with the **G** note:

G   A   B   C   D   E   F   G

The intervals at the moment are: tone, tone, semitone, tone, tone, semitone, tone. The interval between the 6th and 7th notes should be a tone, and the interval between the 7th and 8th notes should be a semitone. By making the **F** note **F♯** instead, the correct intervals are produced. (If the **E** note was made **E♭**, the interval between the 6th and 7th notes would be right, but not the one between the 5th and 6th notes.)

In theory there could be seventeen different major scales: **A, A♯/B♭, B, C, C♯/D♭, D, D♯/E♭, E, F, F♯/G♭, G** and **G♯/A♭**. In practice, only those scales that involve up to five sharp or flat notes are generally used. These are the major scales of **A, B♭, B, C, D♭, D, E♭, E, F, G** and **A♭**. Try writing another of these scales – the **F** major scale, for example. First write all seven letters:

F   G   A   B   C   D   E   F

Now work out the intervals between them. The third interval is a tone and should be a semitone. This is corrected by making the **B** note **B♭**. **B♭** to **C** is a tone, so that interval is correct too. Now let's look at two scales that are close in pitch at the same time – the scales of **E♭** major and **E** major. Initially the same letters can be written for them both, except the **E♭** tonic note of course.

E   F♯   G♯   A   B   C♯   D♯   E
E♭   F   G   A♭   B♭   C   D   E♭

In the **E** major scale, **E** to **F** is only a semitone, so the **F** should be sharpened. Then the **G** has to be made sharp too – producing the correct semitone interval between the 3rd and 4th notes, **G♯** to **A**. **A** to **B** is a tone, but the **C** and **D** notes both have to be sharpened to produce tone intervals, leaving the correct semitone from **D** to **E**. The starting note of the **E♭** scale produces the correct tone interval to begin with. Only the **A** and **B** notes need to be flattened to complete the correct **E♭** major scale. Now try working out one or more of the other major scales yourself.

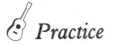

Playing scales on the guitar can be easier than on keyboard instruments because the same pattern and fingering can produce different scales up and down the fretboard. For example, play the **G** major scale – which includes the **F♯** note. The pattern here covers two octaves:

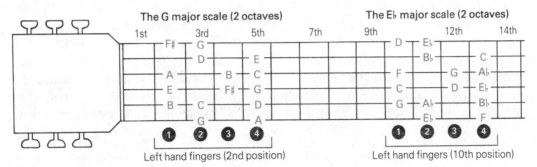

The G major scale (2 octaves)   The E♭ major scale (2 octaves)

Left hand fingers (2nd position)   Left hand fingers (10th position)

Hold your left-hand fingers in what is known as the '2nd position'. This is where the first finger is positioned at and plays notes on the 2nd fret, with the other fingers poised over and taking the notes on the other frets along the fretboard as shown. To play other major scales, move the pattern up or down the fretboard, i.e. the **E♭** major scale, shown above, has its tonic note on the 11th fret, and the scale pattern is played with the left hand in the 10th position. Similarly, the **C** major scale with its tonic on the 8th fret of the 6th string can be played with the same pattern and the hand in the 7th fret position.

5th string patterns

Guitarists may not want to play scales and notes up near the guitar body for reasons of fingering or tonal qualities. Starting the scale on the 5th string instead of the 6th can allow you to play the notes lower down the fretboard. Here is the **D** major scale, for example:

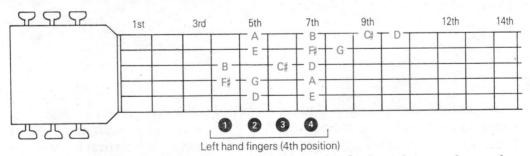

Left hand fingers (4th position)

This pattern can also be moved up and down the fretboard to produce other major scales, i.e. start with the C note on the 3rd fret of the 5th string for the C major scale, or the 6th fret for the E♭ major scale. Scales are worth practising for finger dexterity, knowledge of the notes on the fretboard, finding melodies (the expected notes in a melody are those in the major scale), finding chord shapes and improving lead lines.

Harmony

Melody means consecutive notes – a series of 'dominant' notes that catch our attention more than others. Harmony means simultaneous notes, i.e. notes other than the melody played at the same time as the melody notes. Our ears expect harmony notes to come from the major scale of the tonic note, just as they expect the melody to be drawn from it. When a melody in the key of **C** major, for example, is harmonized, both harmony and melody notes are expected to come from the **C** major scale, i.e. **C D E F G A** and **B**. Should the music be written in the key of **A** major, then the notes will be drawn from that scale, i.e. **A, B, C♯, D, E, F♯** and **G♯**. Here is 'Amazing Grace' again, this time with a harmony:

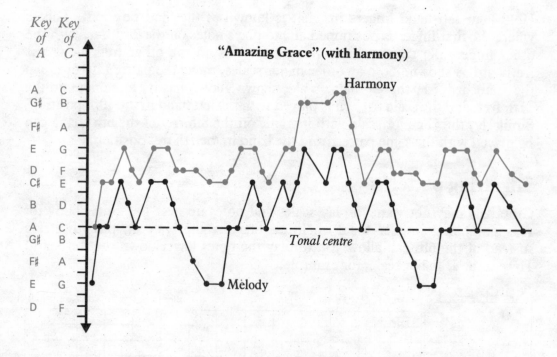

The harmony shown here is slightly higher in pitch than the melody. All the harmony notes, like the melody notes, are from the major scale of the tonic note. The notes of the **C** major scale are shown next to the vertical pitch line – these are the melody and harmony notes when the music is written in the key of **C** major. When the music is in the key of **A** major, the **A** major scale notes apply – these are shown on the left of the **C** scale notes.

Here are both melody and harmony lines of 'Amazing Grace' in the key of **C** major – as shown in graph form on the previous page – together with the words of the first verse. The numbers indicate which string the note is on – all notes are either open strings or on the first three frets. Use the same string as before where no number is shown. Play the melody first, then the harmony. Finally, play the two parts together.

Harmony	5 4		3 4		3 .		4				*String*
	C E	E	G F E		G		G F	F	F	E	*Note*
Melody	6 5		4	5	4			5	3	6	*String*
	G C	C	E D C		E		E D	C	A	G	*Note*
	A –	maz– ing			grace,	how		sweet	the sound		

		3		4	3	2	
	E F	G	G F E		G	G B	B
	5		4	5	4		3
	G C	C	E D C		E	D E	G
	That	saved	a		wretch	like	me

			3	4	3	4	
B C	C	A G E		G		G F	F	F	E
4 3			4	5	4		5		6
E G	G	E D C		E		E D	C	A	G
I	once	was		lost,	but	now	am	found

	3			4	3	4
E G	G	G F E		G	F	E
	5		4	5	4		5
G C	C	E D C		E	D	C
Was	blind,	but		now	I	see

Notice that all the notes from *both* melody and harmony are from the **C** major scale, i.e. just seven notes, **C D E F G A** and **B** (and their octaves).

Now change the music to the key of **A** major – start with the **E** note at the 2nd fret of the 4th string, then find the other notes by following the diagram on the previous page. You'll see that the music sounds basically the same, it's just pitched at a different level. If you need some help finding or playing the notes, listen to the demonstration on the matching cassette.

Chordal accompaniment

A melody is said to be accompanied when instruments provide a background of rhythm and harmony which normally involves chords. A chord is produced when three or more notes are sounded together. The chord notes will either be the same as the melody or harmonize with it. Like melody and vocal harmony parts, chordal accompaniments are 'expected' to include only notes from the major scale of the tonic note.

Three main chords

Chords are used to compose and accompany songs. Three main chords provide a basis for the accompaniment of most songs – for much traditional and country material, only these are needed. In the key of **C** major, the three main chords are **C** (major), **F** (major) and **G** (major). The 'major' is in brackets because major chords are normally referred to by their letter name only.

Chord formation

Simple chords like **C**, **F** and **G** consist of three notes. The fundamental note of a chord is its 'root' note – which the chord is built on and which gives its name to the chord. The root notes of the three main chords in each key are found in the 1st, 4th and 5th positions of the tonic note major scale, while the other chord notes are taken from *alternate* scale notes:

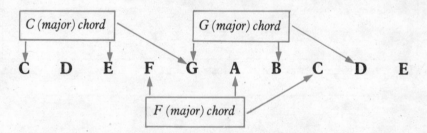

To find the notes of the **C** chord, you take the root **C** note, miss the next note (**D**), take the **E** note, miss the next note (**F**), and take the **G** note. Thus the **C** (major) chord consists of **C**, **E** and **G** notes. The **F** and **G** chord notes are found in the same way. Now write down the **A** major scale and work out the notes of the three main chords in that key.

Octave notes

In practice, the root note doesn't have to be lower in pitch than the others, and the other notes can be lower or higher than each other too. Also, these simple chords often include five or six notes when played – different octaves of the same note are used to fill out and strengthen the chord sound.

The three main chords in the key of **C** major are **C**, **F** and **G**:

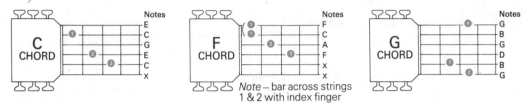

Note – bar across strings
1 & 2 with index finger

Place your left-hand fingers as shown – **❶** = index, **❷** = middle, **❸** = ring, **❹** = little. Strum each chord from bass to treble – don't play strings marked with an 'x'. Strings with no finger indication are played open. The three chords above include only the notes of the **C** major scale – **C D E F G A** and **B**. Notice that guitar chords may involve five or six notes but only three different names.

Accompanying 'Amazing Grace'

You need only three chords to accompany 'Amazing Grace'. Do a heavier downstrum plus two lighter ones for each chord symbol.

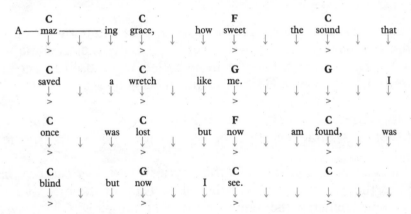

When you've played 'Amazing Grace' in the key of **C** major, try it in **A** major – substitute the **A** chord for the **C**, the **D** for the **F**, and the **E** for the **G**:

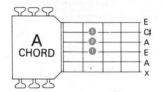 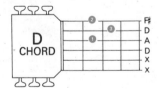 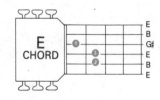

Notice that the notes in the **A**, **D** and **E** chords are all from the **A** major scale. Though the open 6th string **E** note could be played as part of the **A** chord, guitarists generally strum down from the 5th string root note **A**. The same thing applies to the **D** chord in the case of the open 5th string **A** note.

Minor chords

Simple three-note major chords can be described as the most 'normal' sounding of chords. Other simple three-note chords formed by taking alternate notes from the major scale are called 'minor' chords. They have a rather sad sound about them because the interval between the root and next note is only three semitones rather than the four semitone interval of the major chord. Three other commonly used chords in the key of **C** major are **Dm** (**D** minor), **Em** (**E** minor) and **Am** (**A** minor):

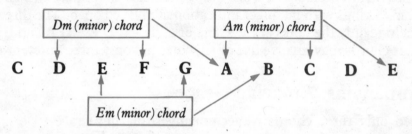

Expected chords

You've seen that simple chords are built on each scale note by taking alternate notes from the major scale. Some of these chords are major, some minor. A summary of the chords that might be expected to be used to accompany a melody written in the key of **C** major is shown below:*

C	**Dm**	**Em**	**F**	**G**	**Am**
1 = major	2 = minor	3 = minor	4 = major	5 = major	6 = minor

Because the key system is arranged the way it is, each key can be considered more or less the 'same' – provided the relationship of the melody or accompaniment notes remains the same, a piece of music can be played quite satisfactorily at different levels of pitch, i.e. in various keys. This means the expected major and minor chords will follow the same order, whatever the key – the chord built on the first note of the scale will always be a major chord, the one built on the second note will be a minor chord, the third a minor chord, the fourth a major chord, and so on. Here are the expected chords for the key of **A** major, for example:

A	**Bm**	**C#m**	**Dm**	**E**	**F#m**
1	2	3	4	5	6

Now write down the expected chords for other keys – the keys of **E♭** major and **D** major, for example, and then work out their notes.

*The chord built on the seventh note of the scale (**Bm♭5** here) is rarely used.

The three minor chords formed from the alternate notes of the **C** major scale
are **Dm**, **Em** and **Am**.

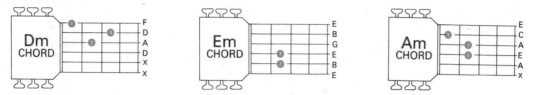

Major and minor chords from the tonic scale are often used together in song
accompaniments. Try playing this chord sequence that was used in many pop
songs of the fifties, as in 'Diana' by Paul Anka. Space the downstrums evenly,
stressing the first of every four, as indicated.

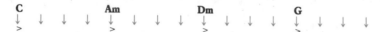

I Want to Hold Your Hand THE BEATLES

Early Beatles songs made imaginative and melodic use of major and minor
chords – 'I Want to Hold Your Hand', for example:

C ↓ ↓ ↓ ↓ G ↓ ↓ ↓ ↓ Am ↓ ↓ ↓ ↓ Em ↓ ↓ ↓ ↓
  >   >   >   >

C ↓ ↓ ↓ ↓ G ↓ ↓ ↓ ↓ Am ↓ ↓ ↓ ↓ Em ↓ ↓ ↓ ↓
  >   >   >   >

F ↓ G ↓ C ↓ Am ↓ F ↓ G ↓ C ↓ ↓ ↓
  >   >   >   >

Woman JOHN LENNON

The first six bars of 'Woman' involve all six chords formed from the major
scale – three major, three minor. In the key of **D** major, these are **D**, **Em**, **F♯m**,
G, **A**, and **Bm**. You haven't seen the **F♯m** and **Bm** chords yet:

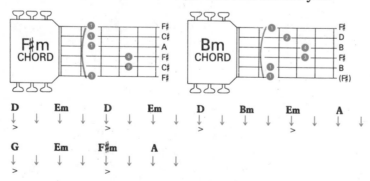

D ↓ Em ↓ D ↓ Em ↓ D ↓ Bm ↓ Em ↓ A ↓
  >   >   >   >

G ↓ ↓ Em ↓ F♯m ↓ A ↓
  >   >

Extended chords – 7ths

The major and minor chords you've seen so far consist of three notes. When a chord has more than three notes, it can be called an 'extended chord'. Chords can be extended by adding more alternate notes from the major scale of the tonic note. The most used extended chords are those that have one extra note – these are called '7th chords'. There are three types of 7th chord, the major 7th (maj7 for short), the minor 7th (m7) and the dominant 7th (7).

Formation of 7th chords

The major chords built on the notes in the 1st and 4th positions of the major scale become major 7th chords when extended by one note:

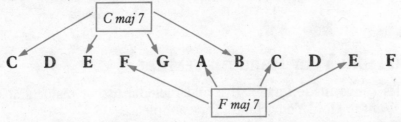

The chord built on the note in the fifth position of the scale becomes a 'dominant 7th' because the added note is only ten semitones above the root note of the chord (the notes added to the first and fourth position chords are eleven semitones above the root):

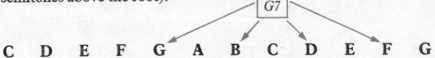

The minor chords built on the second, third and sixth position notes all become minor 7th (m7) chords when a note is added:

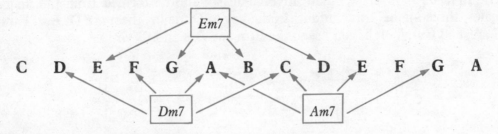

Expected 7th chords

The expected seventh chords in the key of **C** major, shown and analysed above, can be summarized like this: **Cmaj7, Dm7, Em7, Fmaj7, G7, Am7**. 7th chords in other keys will follow the same order as those in the key of **C** .

Here are simple positions for the 7th chords in the key of **C** major:

7th chords can be used to add a more interesting or sophisticated, jazzy flavour to songs. 'Moon River' and 'Don't It Make My Brown Eyes Blue', for example, can start with this sequence: **Cmaj7, Am7, Dm7** and **G7**. You'll notice the similarity between this and the one given on page 33. Not all songs will suit extended chords, but even folk or country accompaniments can involve major and minor 7th chords – as well as the commonly used dominant 7th. The verse of 'Leaving On a Jet Plane', for example, could be played with two major 7th chords plus the dominant 7th at the end. In the key of **C** this would mean **Cmaj7** and **Fmaj7** plus **G7**. 'Everybody's Talkin'', from the film *Midnight Cowboy*, involves the tonic chord alternating with the major 7th at the start – **C** to **Cmaj7** in the key of C.

Ain't Misbehavin' FATS WALLER

Jazz songs are particularly suited to major 7th chords, as well as the other 7ths. Try this chord sequence for the verse of 'Ain't Misbehavin''.

Cmaj₇   Dm₇   Em₇   Am₇   Fmaj₇
↓ ↓ ↓ ↓   ↓ ↓ ↓ ↓   ↓ ↓   ↓ ↓   ↓ ↓ ↓ ↓

Em₇   Am₇   Dm₇   G₇   Cmaj₇   G₇
↓ ↓   ↓ ↓   ↓ ↓   ↓ ↓ ↓ ↓ ↓ ↓   ↓ ↓   ↓ ↓

Tonight's the Night ROD STEWART

Pop songs can also involve extended chords – the chorus of 'Tonight's The Night', for example:

Cmaj₇   Fmaj₇   Cmaj₇   Am₇
↓ ↓ ↓ ↓   ↓ ↓ ↓ ↓   ↓ ↓ ↓ ↓   ↓ ↓ ↓ ↓

Dm₇   Fmaj₇   Cmaj₇   G₇
↓ ↓ ↓ ↓   ↓ ↓ ↓ ↓   ↓ ↓ ↓ ↓   ↓ ↓ ↓ ↓

Minor keys

The major scale is the basis for most western music today, as well as the starting point for analysis. Some music, however, is based on a different scale – the minor scale. It has the same number of notes as the major scale, but the intervals are different. The changed order of intervals in relation to the tonic note makes music in a minor key sound slightly more melancholy or 'laid back' than that in a major key.

The A minor scale

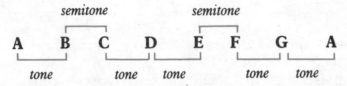

When music is written in the key of **A** minor, its tonic note is **A** (like **A** major), but the notes of the melody and accompaniment are 'expected' to be drawn from the notes above (as opposed to the **A, B, C♯, D, E, F♯** and **G♯** of the **A** major scale), and the accompaniment will end on an **Am** rather than **A** chord.

Expected chords

Chords are formed by taking alternate notes from the minor scale in the same way as the chords were formed from the major scale. You may have noticed a certain similarity between the notes in the **A** minor scale and those in the **C** major scale – yes, they're the same. In fact the key of **A** minor is said to be 'relative' to the key of **C** major because the intervals between the notes are the same, just in a different order. This means the expected chords are the same as those in **C** major (as in the key of **C** major, the chord built on the **B** note is not often used):

Am   **C**   **Dm**   **Em**   **F**   **G**

(or **E**)

You will often come across the **E** or **E7** chord in accompaniments for songs in the key of **A** minor. This is because composers preferred the change of a semitone from **G♯** to **A** rather than the tone change from **G** natural to **A**. Thus the 'natural' minor scale is often altered by making the seventh note a semitone sharper. This means minor keys will involve the same dominant chord built on the fifth note of the scale as the major scale with the same tonic note, i.e. in both keys of **A** major *and* **A** minor, the **E** (or **E7**) chord will be used.

The tonic note of a minor key is always three semitones lower than the tonic note of its relative major key. Work out the relative minor key to the **G** major scale. Which chords are expected in this minor key?

Here are chordal accompaniments for several well-known songs that were written in a minor key. Playing these sequences will help to give you a feel for the structure of minor key melodies and accompaniments.

Greensleeves TRADITIONAL

Do three downstrums for each chord symbol shown below:

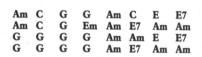

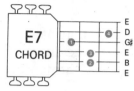

Notice the use of the dominant **E** and **E7** chords instead of the 'natural' **Em**.

Geordie TRADITIONAL

I've used the key of **E** minor for this traditional tune. The 'natural' 5th position chord in this key is **Bm**. For a stronger resolution, the **B7** chord is borrowed from the key of **E** major at the end of the verse (which includes the **D♯** note). Stress every other strum as shown. If you're not sure of the melody, listen to the matching cassette.

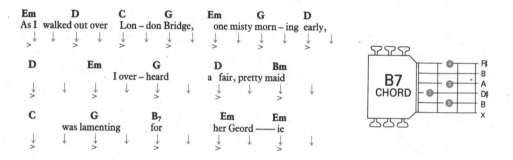

I Shot The Sheriff BOB MARLEY

Bob Marley's big reggae hit is written in a minor key. Here the chords are made up of notes only from the natural minor scale (of **A** minor):

Verse	F Em Am F Em Am	

F   Em₇   Am   Am   Am

Chorus Am   Dm   Am   Am

Summary of the key system

It's important for you to understand the essence of the key system in western music – each key is essentially the 'same' as any other, it's just fixed at a different level of pitch. This is because the relationship of the other scale notes to the tonic or key note is the same in every key, as demonstrated by the general scale doh ray me fah soh lah te doh. Here is a point-by-point summary of what has been covered in this section:

1 The tonic or key note of a piece of music is the note round which the melody 'revolves'. It is the main note with which the other notes have specific relationships, and the note on which the listener expects the melody to finish.

2 Our conditioned ears 'expect' only those notes in the major scale of the tonic note (or the minor scale in minor keys) to be used for melody and accompaniment – just seven notes and their octaves.

3 Each major key involves scale notes with these intervals between them: tone/tone/semitone/tone/tone/tone/semitone. Each major key has a relative minor key three semitones below in pitch, i.e. **C** major and **A** minor. The (natural) minor scale has these intervals between notes: tone/semitone/tone/tone/semitone/tone/tone. The seventh note from the major scale is often used in melodies and accompaniment chords instead of the minor scale seventh, i.e. **G♯** instead of **G** in the key of **A** minor.

4 Chords are used as a basis for composition, accompaniment and analysis of modern music and songs. Chords expected in a particular key are made up from alternate notes of the tonic major scale. Simple major and minor chords consist of three notes, extended 7th chords have four.

5 The chords expected in each major key are built on each note of the tonic major scale, and always follow this order: major/minor/minor/major/major/minor/minor ♭5. (The last is not often used.) The chords expected from the tonic minor scale are: minor/minor ♭5/major/minor/minor/major/major. The frequent use of the sharpened seventh note in minor keys means the chord built on the fifth note of the tonic minor scale becomes a major instead of minor, i.e. **Em** becomes **E** in the key of **A** minor.

Variations

Though our ears expect the seven notes of the tonic major scale (or minor scale in minor keys), there are a number of variations that we now accept in modern music. Temporary key changes and passing notes and chords are necessary to provide more variety to the standard music system and to produce music that isn't too predictable – our ears will accept the greater tension that some changes create, and in fact we enjoy it. Many of the different possibilities for using out-of-key notes and chords are shown in Appendix 1, page 125.

Guitarists tend to favour the keys that involve easier chord fingerings. These happen to be the key of **C** major and four of the keys with sharp notes – **A, D, E** and **G**. A summary of the expected chords (and therefore notes too) in these keys is given below, with the exception of the chords built on the seventh note of each scale. You've seen all of them apart from **G♯m, C♯m** and **B**. Move the **F♯m** up two frets to produce the **G♯m** chord, the **Bm** up two frets for the **C♯m**, and you can use the **B7** instead of the **B**.

Key	Scale note position ('degree') of root note					
	1	2	3	4	5	6
A	A	Bm	C♯m	D	E	F♯m
C	C	Dm	Em	F	G	Am
D	D	Em	F♯m	G	A	Bm
E	E	F♯m	G♯m	A	B	C♯m
G	G	Am	Bm	C	D	Em

Play through the chords of each key one way, then back again. Then extend them all to 7ths – work out the note you have to add and try to find a way of fitting it into the simple major or minor chord shape. Listen to the effect of the different chords and how they relate to the tonic note or chord.

Transposing with the capo

The key of a song often needs to be altered to suit the pitch of a singer or the playing abilities of the guitarist – this is called 'transposing'. The capo can change keys quickly and easily. Electric guitarists use the capo only occasionally, but acoustic guitarists like to use it to change key and still maintain an 'open' sound. It also helps them to use the same tricks that they've developed by keeping the same familiar chord shapes. By clamping across the guitar neck and pressing all the strings down at one fret, the capo raises the string pitch by the fret number it's placed on. With the capo on the 2nd fret and using the **G**, **C** and **D** chord shapes, for example, you're actually playing **A**, **D** and **E** chords and the key has gone up from **G** to **A**.

Transposing without the capo

On page 27 we looked at movable major scale patterns. There are also movable chord shapes, some of which you've already used. These movable shapes are important for the guitarist to understand and play, especially when transposing songs and arrangements from one key to another. These are examined later in the arranging section towards the end of the book.

THE VISUAL MUSIC SYSTEM – PITCH

The stave

The visual music system needs to show the pitch of notes and how long they are to be sounded. During the Middle Ages, monks transcribing hymns began to indicate the pitch of notes with small signs above the words to show falling or rising pitch – these helped them to remember the melody more easily. Then they placed the signs on horizontal lines to indicate relative pitch more precisely. This led to our present system, which involves the use of five horizontal lines – known as a 'stave'.

The treble clef

When a sign is placed at the start of the stave, it fixes the pitch of the notes that are written on it – then the stave becomes a 'clef'. There are two clefs used in sheet music today, the bass and treble clefs. The treble clef is used for both song melodies and the right-hand part for the pianist. It is also used for six-string guitar music.

G Note

The sign for the treble clef is an old version of the letter 'G'. It circles the second line from the bottom, and indicates that a note written on this line will be a **G** note. The positions of all the other notes are then fixed in relation to the **G** note. Moving up the page towards the top line of the clef means going up in pitch and up the alphabet; moving down the clef means going down the alphabet and down in pitch.

Notes on the treble clef

D E F G A B C D E F G   ↑ up in pitch

All note signs are circular like those shown above, but they vary slightly to indicate different time values. This will be looked at later.

Play the open 3rd string on your guitar. This note is the **G** note that should be sounded when a note is marked on the second to bottom line of the treble clef. Unison **G** notes (i.e. notes of exactly the same pitch, in other positions on the fretboard) could of course be played instead:

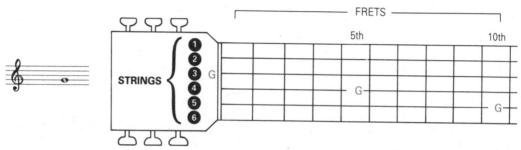

Treble clef notes on the guitar

Because notes of the same pitch can be found in several places on the guitar fretboard, guitarists can play the notes of the treble clef in several different ways. Here is one common way, using the lowest possible positions on the fretboard – and therefore including some open string notes:

	D	E	F	G	A	B	C	D	E	F	G
String	4	4	4	3	3	2	2	2	1	1	1
Fret	0	2	3	0	2	0	1	3	0	1	3

Thus the **D** note marked below the lowest line of the treble clef can be produced by playing the open 4th string, the **E** note by playing the 2nd fret of the 4th string, and so on. Two other ways of playing the same treble clef notes are shown below. The first involves only the 4th string, while the second uses low position fretted notes without open strings.

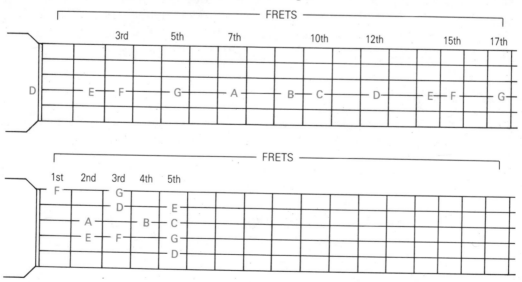

Leger lines

Most notes in a melody are likely to lie somewhere on the stave, but some may be higher or lower than the range of pitch covered by the five lines. Rather than switching to a different clef, leger lines are used above and below the stave:

The notes follow on down or up in the usual way from the notes on the stave. The leger lines add another two or so octaves to the possible range of pitch that can be covered.

Sharp or flat notes

You've seen that five of the twelve semitone notes making up each octave are called either sharp or flat: **A♯** or **B♭**, **C♯** or **D♭**, **D♯** or **E♭**, **F♯** or **G♭**, **G♯** or **A♭**. These sharp or flat notes can be indicated on the stave by placing a sign *before* the note:

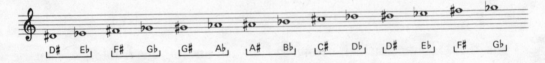

Remember that both notes in each pair are exactly the same pitch.

When a sharp or flat sign is placed next to a note as shown above, it means that the note is not 'expected' in the key, i.e. it is not from the scale of the tonic or key note. These out-of-key notes are called 'accidentals'. The sharp or flat notes that *are* expected, i.e. those that are in the scale of the tonic note, are shown in a different way – as explained on the next theory page.

The natural sign

A natural sign (♮) cancels the effect of a flat or sharp sign that has been indicated before. More information on the use of the natural sign is given later.

Pages 40 and 41 showed the natural notes on the five lines of the treble clef. Several string and fret positions were given for these notes. Now you can add higher and lower leger line notes as well as the intermediate notes.*

Ascending semitones

Play the notes going up in pitch first, with the intermediate notes all shown as sharps. The string and fret positions shown below the notation are the lowest possible on the fretboard. You begin with the open 6th string **E** note, the lowest note on the guitar.

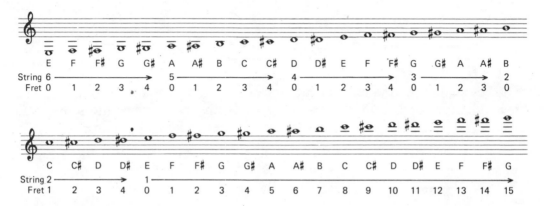

Descending semitones

Now play the notes coming down in pitch, with the intermediate notes shown as flats. This time try the different set of string and fret positions given.

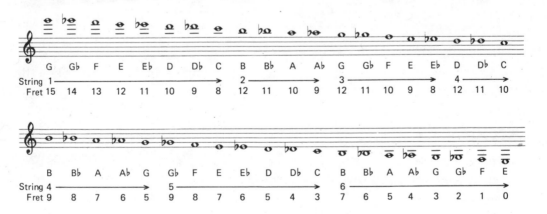

*The guitar sounds an octave lower than it is actually written – see 'Transposing instruments' on page 123.

Key signatures

You've seen that in all keys except **C** (and **A** minor), one or more altered notes are expected. Those sharp or flat notes that are part of the tonic scale, i.e. in key, are indicated at the start of each line of music. This avoids cluttering the music with sharp or flat signs, and shows the key more clearly. Though shown on one line or space only, each sharp or flat sign of a key signature applies to all notes of the same name, whatever octave. When music is written in the key of **G** major, for example, a ♯ sign is placed on the top line to show that all **F** notes should be played sharp:

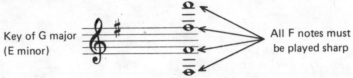

The key signature for a minor key is the same as for its relative major key. The key signature for **E** minor is the same as **G** major, **B** minor the same as **D** major, and so on. Here are the other common keys with sharp notes:

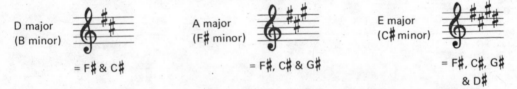

These are the key signatures for the more popular keys with flat notes:

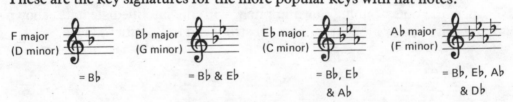

Musicians recognize key signatures, and by knowing immediately what key the music is written in, they are able to read and assimilate it more quickly.

Accidentals

On page 42 I explained that a sharp or flat sign placed to the left of a note means it is altered from the pitch expected in the key, i.e. the note is not sharp or flat in the major scale of the tonic note. A note altered in this way is called an 'accidental' – a **C** note with a ♯ placed next to it when the music is in the key of **G** major, for example. Similarly, the 'natural' sign (♮) is used to cancel a sharp or flat sign in the key signature. A note altered in this way is also an accidental – a **C** note with a natural sign next to it in the key of **A** major, for example.

In this section you've seen how notes are written on the treble clef, and how to find them on the guitar. To help you put into practice what you've learnt, we're going to look at two songs you've seen before.

Amazing Grace   *(Pitch Only)*

The melody notes of 'Amazing Grace' were given on page 29, but I want you to write the melody an octave higher than given there. To get you started, here's the first line:

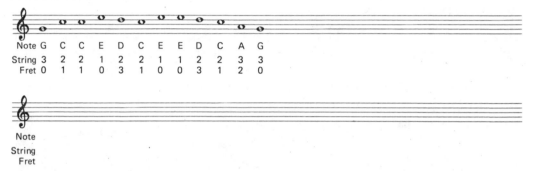

Note	G	C	C	E	D	C	E	E	D	C	A	G
String	3	2	2	1	2	2	1	1	2	2	3	3
Fret	0	1	1	0	3	1	0	0	3	1	2	0

Note
String
Fret

When you've completed the melody, put the correct string and fret numbers below each note and play the whole tune while reading the treble clef notes.

Greensleeves   *(Pitch only)*

On page 37 you accompanied this song with chords in the key of **A** minor. I've used the key of **E** minor here, which has the same key signature as **G** major – one sharp note, **F♯**. The first few notes have string and fret numbers below them – work out and write down the positions for the others. For the second half of the verse I've shown string numbers only – work out the fret numbers and write the notes on the treble clef. Notice the **D♯** in the melody, the sharpened seventh note borrowed from the **E** major scale, and also the **C♯** – sometimes the sixth note of the minor scale is sharpened to 'match' the sharpened seventh note.

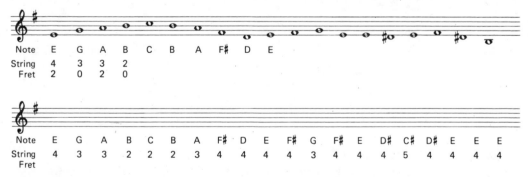

Note	E	G	A	B	C	B	A	F♯	D	E
String	4	3	3	2						
Fret	2	0	2	0						

Note	E	G	A	B	C	B	A	F♯	D	E	F♯	G	F♯	E	D♯	C♯	D♯	E	E	E
String	4	3	3	2	2	2	3	4	4	4	4	3	4	4	4	5	4	4	4	4
Fret																				

The two melodies above are demonstrated on the matching cassette.

The Bass clef

In today's sheet music, as well as in many songbooks, you'll come across music written on the bass clef. A keyboard arrangement is put together by a pianist who tries to include all the important elements of the song on three staves – the melody on the first, the higher accompaniment notes on the second (for the right hand to play), and the lower accompaniment notes on the third (for the left hand to play). The top two staves use the treble clef, which we've already looked at, but the lowest stave involves the bass part of the song and is written on the bass clef.

The notes to be played by the pianist's left hand represent the bass part of the music, so they are consistently lower than the melody or right-hand accompaniment. Rather than have all the notes on leger lines stretching down below the five lines of the treble clef, another clef is used – the bass clef. The pitch of the bass clef notes is set by the bass clef sign at the start of each line – this old version of an 'F' fixes the **F** note on the second line from the top:

F Note

The other notes of the bass clef will follow naturally from the **F** note, like this:

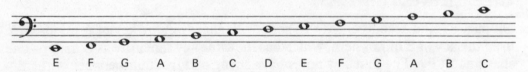

E   F   G   A   B   C   D   E   F   G   A   B   C

Leger lines can be used in the same way as they were with the treble clef – as for the low **E** and high **C** notes shown above. Key signatures and 'accidentals' are indicated on the bass clef in a similar way too.

Range of pitch – bass and treble clefs

The **C** note on the leger line immediately above the five lines of the bass clef is the same pitch as the **C** note on the leger line immediately below the treble clef:

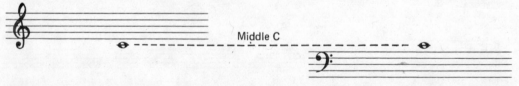

Middle C

This **C** note is aptly named 'middle C' – it comes between the treble and bass clefs as shown above, as well as lying roughly in the middle of piano and other keyboards.

Bass guitar note positions

One set of fretboard positions for bass clef notes is given below. 4 = the lowest string on the bass guitar, and 1 the highest. The 6-string guitarist can play these notes on the four lower strings, though they'll be one octave higher, i.e. where 4 is given, play the 6th string, where 1, play the 3rd string. The same fret positions can be used.

Being able to read notes on the bass clef will help the 6-string guitarist interpret sheet music more fully, i.e. work out the exact chord being played, runs being used and ideas for rhythm patterns. This will help in arranging the music for solo guitar as well, of course, for playing in a band.

Sample song bass lines *(Pitch Only)*

I'll be dealing with rhythm in the next section, but playing these few samples, taken from sheet music, will help you to learn the bass clef:

Careless Whisper

Chord root notes are normally used when a chord is first played.

Lessons in Love

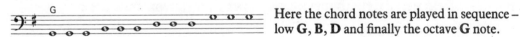

Here the chord notes are played in sequence – low **G**, **B**, **D** and finally the octave **G** note.

Rockin' all over the World

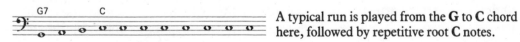

A typical run is played from the **G** to **C** chord here, followed by repetitive root **C** notes.

Rock around the Clock

This song has strong ties to blues music, so it includes a flattened 'blue' note – **G** natural. The natural sign cancels the ♯ in the key signature.

THE VISUAL MUSIC SYSTEM – RHYTHM

Beats

Rhythm involves not only the time value of notes (i.e. how long they last), but also the stress placed on them. A piece of music needs to be broken up into manageable sections so that the musician can interpret it more easily and quickly. Because all music has what can be called an 'underlying stress pattern', there are natural divisions that occur. One of these divisions is beats.

Some notes are stressed more than others, and these notes are said to be 'on the beat', i.e. where we would naturally tap our feet. A simple example of the division of notes into stressed and unstressed notes is shown above. There are ten notes of equal length joined in pairs. The first note of each pair is on the beat and stressed more than the other. Tap your foot as you say a loud 'on' for these notes. When your foot has risen to its highest point before coming back down for the next beat note, say a soft 'off'. Beats come at regular intervals, so keep the beat notes evenly spaced. (Allow about a second between them.)

Bars

The underlying stress pattern of music means that notes on the beat are stressed more than notes off the beat. It also means that some of the beats will be stressed more than the others. These stronger beats come at regular intervals. Here is one possible stress pattern (with just one note per beat shown this time):

The first of every three beats is stressed more than the following two. This underlying stress pattern allows us to divide music into larger segments, making it easier to read and interpret. These segments are called bars. Bars are shown by vertical lines across the stave, which come just before the heavier beat:

Off-the-beat notes are included again in the example above. Each beat is stressed, but the first of every three is stressed more – tap your foot more heavily on these, and say the 'on' a bit louder. Remember to keep the beats evenly spaced.

Playing on- and off-beat notes

The natural underlying stress pattern of music involves beats. Notes played *on* the beat, whether strummed, plucked or picked out individually, will normally be stressed more than notes *off* the beat. On pages 31, 33, 35 and 37, you played evenly spaced downstrums. Normally when strings (or a string) are struck in a downward direction the notes are on the beat, and indeed all the downstrums you played across the chords were on the beat. Now we'll include off-beat upstrums, which should be exactly halfway between the beats:

Hold a simple chord like an E (shown on page 31), and strum down/up for each beat. The upstrums should be shorter than the downstrums – strum up across just two or three treble strings. Tap your foot on each downstrum, which should be stressed more, i.e. played louder than the upstrums. As your foot reaches its highest point before coming down for the next beat, do the upstrum – the beats/downstrums must be evenly spaced, with the upstrums coming *exactly* halfway between them. Keep doing down/up strums over and over again, as smoothly as you can. If you have a metronome, set it about ♩ = 60, and use it throughout this section. Each click represents a beat.

Strong beats

The underlying stress pattern of a piece of music means that some beats are stressed more than others. These emphasized beats are regularly spaced and occur in written music immediately after each vertical bar line – and notes on these beats are normally stressed more. Here is a familiar rhythm pattern:

Hold a chord and stress the first downstrum of each bar – your flatpick or fingers could go across more strings and play this downstrum louder. Tap your foot on each beat/downstrum, and keep them evenly spaced. Now include off-beat upstrums in the pattern. Stress each downstrum more than the upstrums, and emphasize the first downstrum in each bar more than the other two:

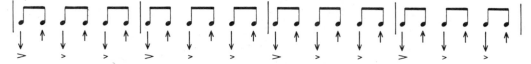

Rhythm patterns

The underlying stress patterns in music mean there will be stronger beats occurring at regular intervals. Perhaps the simplest rhythmic pattern is the three-beat type – which in fact you played on the previous page.

The 3-beat (waltz) rhythm

When the stress pattern involves extra emphasis on the first of three beats, the rhythm produced is easily recognizable as a waltz rhythm. Counting the beats will makes the three-beat pattern clearer:

When off-beat notes are included, the pattern can be counted like this:

The 4–beat (common) rhythm

Most music today is written in what is known as 'common time'. This involves four beats to the bar, i.e. the first of every *four* beats is stressed more heavily than the others:

With off-beat notes added, the four-beat rhythm pattern would be counted like this:

The rhythm patterns above represent the underlying stress patterns of most of today's music. Melody notes (and even accompaniment notes) do not necessarily come on every beat, but the stress pattern is 'felt underneath the music' as it is played. Over the next few pages we'll be looking at different examples of accompaniments and melodies to illustrate rhythm patterns and structure.

On pages 31, 33, 35 and 37, you played simple downstrum accompaniments for eight songs. Most involved a heavy strum every four beats (common time), two involved a heavy strum every three beats (waltz time), and for one, every other strum was stressed (marching time):

Common time (4 beats per bar)	*Waltz time (3 beats per bar)*	*Marching time (2 beats per bar)*
I want to hold your hand	Amazing grace*	Geordie
Woman	Greensleeves	
Ain't misbehavin'*		(This rhythm is looked at later in the section)
Tonight's the night*		
I shot the sheriff		

*These songs have a 'swing' rhythm – see page 84.

Go back to these songs, put in the bar lines and play them again. Use both down and upstrums and count the beats while you're playing.

Picking accompaniment patterns

Songs requiring a gentler approach are often accompanied with picking patterns. Here are two 'arpeggio' patterns, the first for songs with a three-beat rhythm, the second for those with a four-beat rhythm:

```
T   i   m   r   m   i          T  i  m  r  m  i T  i
1 & 2 & 3 &                     1 & 2 & 3 & 4 &
```

T = Right-hand thumb
i = Index finger
m = Middle finger
r = Ring finger

The right-hand thumb strikes a bass string – preferably the root note of the chord – and the index, middle and ring fingers always play the 3rd, 2nd and 1st strings respectively. Emphasize the thumb strike because it's on the first beat of the bar, and play the notes on the other beats a little louder than those between beats. (If you'd prefer to use a flatpick, play the first three notes in a downward direction, and the next three upward – the last two notes of the four-beat pattern can be played down then up.)

More song accompaniments

Use the strumming or picking patterns to accompany the following songs. (Each chord symbol represents one bar.)

Songs with 3-beat rhythm	*Songs with 4-beat rhythm*
Catch The Wind – **G G C C G G C C G G C D G**	Get Back – **E E A E E E A E E E A E**
I Got You Babe – **A A D D A A D G E E₇**	Hey Jude – **G D D G C G D G**
Scarborough Fair – **Am C G Am Am D Am Am**	Let It Be – **C G Am F C G F C**
Annie's Song – **C F G Am F C Em Am**	Mr Tambourine Man – **G A D G D G A A**

Note lengths

You've seen that underlying stress patterns mean music can be broken up into segments called bars, each with the same number of beats. Beats are evenly spaced, as are the heavier beats that begin each bar – thus all the bars of a piece of music will be the same length. You'll see that the time value of notes – how long they last – depends on the number of beats in each bar.★

All notes are round in shape, but their time value or length changes if they are filled in or not, or if they have a stem attached or not. Also, the stem itself may vary and therefore indicate a different length. The four main note signs you'll come across in sheet music are these:

American Name		*English Name*
Whole-note (= 2 half-notes)	o	Semibreve (= 2 minims)
Half-note (= 2 quarter-notes)	𝅗𝅥	Minim (= 2 crotchets)
Quarter-note (= 2 eighth-notes)	𝅘𝅥	Crotchet (= 2 quavers)
Eighth-note	𝅘𝅥𝅮	Quaver

(Two eighth-notes quavers may be joined: 𝅘𝅥𝅮𝅘𝅥𝅮)

The stems may be written up or down, (i.e. 𝅗𝅥 𝅘𝅥 𝅘𝅥𝅮 or 𝅗𝅥 𝅘𝅥 𝅘𝅥𝅮). If a note is higher on the stave, the stem is generally down, and up if lower on the stave. This makes the music easier to read, and doesn't affect the length of the notes.

Notes and beats

On page 50 I mentioned that most of today's popular music is written in 'common time'. This is where there are four beats to the bar. The American note names are based on this rhythm pattern, with the quarter-note representing one beat:

Whole-note	o	= 4 beats or one whole bar in common time
Half-note	𝅗𝅥	= 2 beats or half a bar in common time
Quarter-note	𝅘𝅥	= 1 beat or quarter of a bar in common time
Eighth-note	𝅘𝅥𝅮	= ½ beat or an eighth of a bar in common time

★Speed
No mention has been made of the speed of the music in relation to note lengths. This is because the note signs don't indicate an *absolute* length, just a length *relative* to each other whatever the speed. Sometimes a tempo indication is given before a piece of music, but how fast a song or piece of music is taken may often vary according to the player's judgement and taste.

Before giving you actual melodies, I want you to be sure how to count beats and hold notes over them for the correct length of time. Using just one type of note at a time, let's have a look at the different possibilities in common time – with four beats to the bar. The first possibility is the whole-note (semibreve) which lasts four beats, i.e. the whole bar in common time:

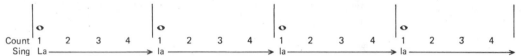

Each beat must be given the same amount of time, i.e. they must be evenly spaced. To help you do this consistently, I've given each beat exactly the same space visually, which will continue throughout this section.

Tap your foot on each beat and hum or 'la' the note when your foot comes down for the first beat. Instead of humming or singing, you could play a note or strum a chord. Do four evenly spaced foot taps, counting 1, 2, 3, 4 to yourself at the same time. Hold the note right through the bar until *immediately before* your foot comes down for the first beat of the second bar. Make sure the note starts exactly on the count of '1' for the first beat and finishes an instant before the first beat of the next bar when you start the next note. The other possibilities in common time are shown below:

Sing, pick a note or strum a chord on the first beat count, tapping your foot as before. The half-note (minim) bars involve each note lasting two full beats, i.e. half the bar each, so stop the first note momentarily before the third beat count. The second note stops just before the first beat of the next bar.

The quarter-note (crotchet) bars involve each note lasting exactly one beat each – so each note starts exactly on the beat count (and foot tap), and ends immediately before the next beat count where the next note begins. In the eighth-note (quaver) bars each note lasts exactly half a beat. Off-beat notes must start exactly halfway between beats – when your foot is at its highest point before coming down to tap on the next beat count.

Time signatures: ⁴₄

A time signature is placed at the start of the first line of music, after the clef sign and key signature. It includes two numbers that indicate the underlying stress pattern of the music. The top number tells us the number of beats in each bar, the lower number the 'time value' or length of each beat:

C or **4 = Four beats per bar**
       4 = One beat has the time value of a quarter-note (crotchet)

A large 'C' is often used instead of ⁴₄, but both these time signatures mean the same thing – common time. Four beats per bar with each beat a quarter-note (crotchet) in length means a total time value of four quarter-notes.

Bars with mixed notes in ⁴₄ time

The four quarter-notes time value of a bar in ⁴₄ time can involve combinations of different notes. Here are some mixed note bars that you will come across:

Tap your foot on each beat count as before, and make sure the beats are evenly spaced. The top example includes half-notes (minims) and quarter-notes (crotchets). The first bar begins with a half-note – 'la' over the first two beats, and then do two more 'las' for the two quarter-notes which follow. Remember that these notes start exactly on the beat count and last right up to where the next note begins. Notice that all the bars above add up to four quarter-notes of time value.

The second example involves quarter-notes (crotchets) and eighth-notes (quavers), the last example includes half-, quarter- and eighth-notes. Make sure the second eighth-note in a beat comes exactly half-way between beat counts. Start the 'la' for these when your foot is at its highest point.

When you can follow the examples above smoothly and correctly, try counting beats and getting note lengths right *as well as* reading and producing the correct pitch for the melodies given on the next page.

Here are parts of two instrumentals and two songs, all in common time, i.e. with four beats per bar and a time signature of **4⁄4** or C. First count the beats and 'la' the notes (just hum any note for this purpose). Once you're happy with the rhythm and note lengths, work out the pitch of the notes and where they are on the guitar. You can play all the notes on the first four frets (and open strings), and I've given you the positions for the first notes. Listen to the matching cassette, or go back to the pitch section (pages 41–45) if necessary.

Study SOR   Start with **C** note, 2nd string 1st fret.

Bill Bailey TRADITIONAL   Start with **D** note, open 4th string

Hungarian Air BATHIOLI   Start with **A** note, 3rd string 2nd fret

Whiskey in the Jar TRADITIONAL   Start with **A** note, 3rd string 2nd fret

There is a one-beat lead-in to 'Whiskey in the Jar'. Count 'four' as you play the first note, and then stress the first beat/note of the full bar.

These pieces are demonstrated on the matching cassette.

The ³4 time signature

On pages 50 and 51 the two main stress patterns in music today were examined. By far the most used rhythm is common time, which you've just looked at, but the next in popularity is waltz time. Both 'Amazing Grace' and 'Greensleeves' involve a three-beat stress pattern, as you saw earlier in the book. The usual time signature for this kind of rhythm is this:

3 = **Three beats per bar**
4 = **One beat has the time value of a quarter-note (crotchet)**

Three beats in a bar and each lasting a quarter-note (crotchet) means the total time value or length of each bar is the equivalent of three quarter-notes. Because the whole-note (semibreve) lasts longer than one bar in ³4 time, whole-notes are never used with this time signature. Because each beat has a time value of a quarter-note the half-, quarter- and eighth-notes last for two beats, one beat, and half a beat respectively – the same as in ⁴4 time. Here are some bars that you will come across in sheet music:

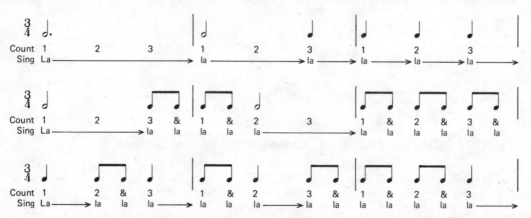

The first bar has a half-note (minim) with a dot next to it. This dot increases its length to three beats from two, so the dotted half-note lasts the whole bar in ³4 time. Dotted notes are dealt with fully on page 66.

Follow the count given beneath each bar, tapping your foot on each beat. Stress the first beat in each bar. Sing or hum the notes as shown, coming in exactly on the beat count and stopping immediately before the next note begins – as you did previously. Keep the beats even and don't go too fast.

When you can follow the examples above, try the song and instrumental examples on the following page.

Here are parts of two classical instrumentals and one traditional song, all in waltz time. That means they all have three beats per bar and the ¾ time signature. As you did for the pieces in ⁴₄, first check the note lengths by tapping your foot on the beats and humming the notes. Then work out the pitch of the notes and where they are on the guitar – as before I've given you the starting note position.

Waltz CARCASSI   Start with **E** and **C** notes, 4th string 2nd fret and 2nd string 1st fret.

This waltz from Carcassi involves notes played at the same time. Sometimes notes played together are joined with one stem, as here. Use your right hand thumb and finger at the same time.

The Wild Rover TRADITIONAL   Start with **A** note, 3rd string 2nd fret

Like 'Whiskey in the Jar', there's a one note lead in for 'The Wild Rover'. Count three for that note and stress the first beat of the first full bar.

Minuet BACH   Start with **D** note, 2nd string 3rd fret

The '1' and '2' mean first and second time through – play the first eight bars up to the double line with two dots (which means repeat the section), then go back to the start and play only the first *six* bars again, followed by the last two.

These pieces are demonstrated on the matching cassette.

Rests

So far you've seen and played 'continuous' music – accompaniment patterns that repeated over and over again without pause, to underpin the melody, then melodies where one note lasts until the next takes over. Though accompaniments tend to be more or less continuous, melody lines generally aren't – there are pauses here and there, either for dramatic effect or variety.

Pauses between notes in music are called rests, and for each note sign there's an equivalent rest sign of the same length:

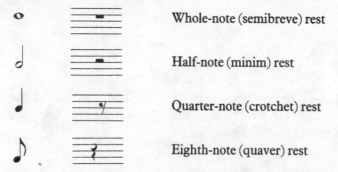

○	Whole-note (semibreve) rest
𝅗𝅥	Half-note (minim) rest
𝅘𝅥	Quarter-note (crotchet) rest
𝅘𝅥𝅮	Eighth-note (quaver) rest

The rest signs have the same relationship with each other as the note signs, i.e. the whole-note (semibreve) rest is twice as long as the half-note (minim) rest, the half-note rest is twice as long as the quarter-note (crotchet) rest, and the quarter-note rest is twice as long as the eighth-note (quaver) rest.

Though the whole-note (semibreve) rest is normally considered to have the same time value or length as the whole-note – as it does when being used as a complete bar's rest in $^4_4$ time – it is also used to denote a complete bar's rest in $^3_4$ and other rhythms.

Rests and beats

To make the time value of each rest sign absolutely clear, here are the rest signs and their length in beats – when they occur in the $^4_4$ and $^3_4$ rhythms:

Whole-note rest		= Complete bar in both $^4_4$ and $^3_4$ time
Half-note rest		= 2 beats in $^4_4$ time (2 quarter-note rests are used in $^3_4$ time for 2 beats' rest)
Quarter-note rest		= 1 beat in $^4_4$ and $^3_4$ time
Eighth-note rest		= ½ beat in $^4_4$ and $^3_4$ time

Now try playing the examples on the next page, which don't include the eighth-note rest. Because they can be more difficult to read and count, eighth-note rests are dealt with on the following double page spread.

The examples from melodies below include occasional rests. Follow the count beneath the notation, and tap your foot on every beat. As usual I've given equal space to each beat, so you have extra visual help to produce the correct note and rest lengths. As a check, listen to the demonstration on the matching cassette.

Scarborough Fair TRADITIONAL　　Start with **A** note, 3rd string 2nd fret

The high **A** notes in the melody of 'Scarborough Fair' – bars 6 and 10 – are found at the 5th fret of the first string. All other notes are on the first three frets or open strings. Notice that the complete bar rest sign is normally placed in the centre of the bar.

Carrickfergus TRADITIONAL　　Start with **D** note, 2nd string 3rd fret

There is a three note/beat lead in for 'Carrickfergus'. Count 'one' to yourself, then play the lead in notes. Stress the first beat in the first full bar.

Eighth-note (quaver) rests in ⁴₄ and ³₄

Almost all of today's popular music is written in ⁴₄ or ³₄ time. The eighth-note (quaver) rest – like the eighth-note itself of course – lasts for only half a beat in these two rhythms, so this makes it a little more difficult to read correctly. When eighth-note rests are used, notes may stop or start in the middle of a beat. Let's go over some examples that you're likely to come across in sheet music:

Keep the foot taps going steadily and evenly as usual, and sing or hum the notes across them. The first bar above has an eighth-note rest on the second beat – stop the note just before you count 'two' and come down with your foot. When your foot reaches its highest point, i.e. half way through the second beat, the next note begins.

Eighth-note rests are more often *on the beat* count in song melodies, with the next melody note coming in on the halfbeat. An eighth-note on the beat *followed* by an eighth-note rest on the halfbeat usually means a 'staccato' or chopped effect – like the notes in the first bar of the second line above, for example. They should be sounded on the beat counts and stopped halfway through the beat when your foot reaches its highest point.

On the following page I've shown some examples of eighth-note rests – you'll see that the staccato-type eighth-notes mentioned above will normally occur when melodies or riffs are played by instruments rather than sung by voices.

Song melodies may be written as a continuous sound, with no rests – as one note ends the next starts. Singers must take breaths occasionally, but the rests are considered so short and incidental they aren't written down. In fact, written music is only an approximation of what is heard, and readers tend to interpret it and change it to suit their own style, judgement or purposes.

Danny Boy TRADITIONAL   Start with **B** note, 5th string 2nd fret

I've included some eighth-note rests here, which tell the reader to stop those notes before the rests, and to have distinct, though short, pauses:

Guitar riffs with damping

A riff is a short musical phrase. Guitar riffs are made more interesting and dynamic by the use of 'damping' – notes are stopped short, usually by the left hand. The pressure is released but the finger remains in contact with the string, stopping it from ringing on. The staccato effect mentioned on the previous page should be produced in the riff below, which involves just fretted notes – so your left hand should stay in the 3rd position throughout:

The opening **G** note is at the 5th fret of the 4th string, the **C** note starting the second bar is at the 5th fret of the 3rd string, and the low **B♭** note near the end is at the 6th fret of the 6th string. Damp notes before each rest. Now try an ending riff with doublestops (two notes together), then a chordal riff. Again, the left hand must damp the strings before the eighth note rests:

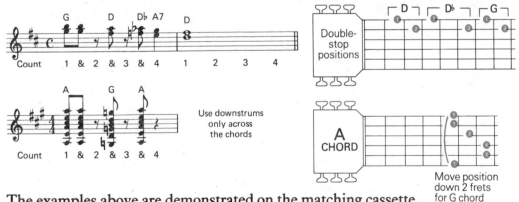

The examples above are demonstrated on the matching cassette.

Ties within a bar

A tie is a curved line connecting two notes of the *same* pitch, which adds the length of the second note to the first. Ties help to make written music clearer and therefore easier to read. Here are two examples:

= time value of 3 eighth-notes (quavers)　　　　= time value of 5 eighth-notes (quavers)

Ties can be used within a single bar and also across bar lines. On this page we'll look at notes between two bar lines that are tied together. Here are some examples in ⁴4 and ³4 time:

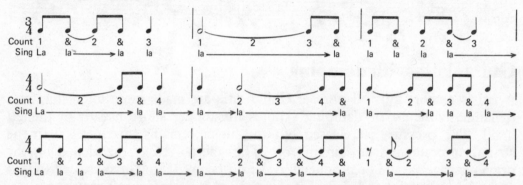

Count the beats very carefully and hold the notes as long as indicated by the 'las' beneath. Keep your foot taps evenly spaced and stop or start the off-beat notes exactly on the halfbeat as before.

Different writing methods

Transcribers of music have their own preferences for indicating note lengths and rhythm. Methods of writing music go through fashions as well, so you may see two (or even several) ways of writing the same bar. For example, the first bar above could have been written:

$\frac{3}{4}$ ♪ ♩ ♪ ♩

1 & 2 & 3

This way of writing the bar doesn't make the three beats of the bar clear, whereas using a tie does. Generally music transcribers will try to make syncopated music (notes stopping and starting on the off-beat) easier to follow by showing the beats of the bar more clearly.

Some ways of using tied notes are shown in the song and instrumental examples on the following page.

Ties are often used when some sort of syncopation is involved, i.e. where a note is advanced from the expected or standard position *on* the beat to the *off*-beat – as in 'Jamaica Farewell' and the blues riff below. They also occur in melody lines where notes on the beat are held longer until the next note begins on the off-beat – as in 'Danny Boy' and 'The Wild Rover'.

Jamaica Farewell TRADITIONAL

The calypso rhythm produces an emphasis or 'push' on the half-beat between the second and third beats – hence the tie there.

The Wild Rover TRADITIONAL *(Mark two)*

Danny Boy TRADITIONAL *(Mark two)*

This time I've removed the rests and used ties:

Lead riff

Hold your left hand in the 3rd position and all the notes can be fretted with the index and ring fingers.

The accidental note is **B♭** (a note in the key of **G** that produces a bluesy sound), and the flat sign next to the first **B** note in the second bar applies to the other **B** note that follows in the same bar.

Ties across bar lines

The notes and rests in each bar must add up to the correct time value for the time signature involved. In $^4_4$, each bar must add up to four quarter notes (crotchets), no more and no less, and each bar in $^3_4$ must total three quarter notes (crotchets). So when a note starts in one bar and has to end in another, a tie must be used to cross the bar line. The length of the note in the second bar must be added to the length of the note in the first. Here are some examples in $^3_4$ and $^4_4$:

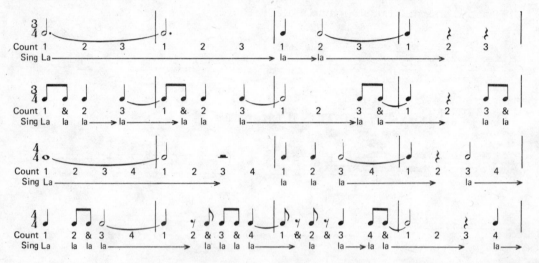

Tap your foot, follow the counts and hum the notes over them as usual. The dotted half-note (minim) in the first bar above lasts three beats, and is then extended for another three beats by the tie to another dotted half-note in the next bar, i.e. the note is held for two bars or six beats/quarter-notes (crotchets). The third bar has a half-note tied to a quarter-note in the fourth bar, so this note lasts for three beats/quarter-notes in total. Add the value of the other tied notes in the same way.

Song and instrumental examples with tied notes are shown on the opposite page.

The rhythm content of written music tends to be an approximation of what is heard, so you may well come across different versions of songs – some that follow the original recording reasonably closely, and others that are more simplified and approximate. Both types are valid as long as the reader gets enough from the written music for his or her purposes. I've changed the version of 'Scarborough Fair' you saw on page 59 slightly, as an illustration of possible variations as well as to give you some practice with ties across bar lines.

Scarborough Fair TRADITIONAL *(Mark two)*

Wonderful Tonight ERIC CLAPTON *(Lead riff)*

Here are the first three bars of the lead guitar riff from 'Wonderful Tonight':

The left hand stays in the 7th position for all three bars, so the index finger holds the **B** note at the 7th fret of the 1st string, the little finger holds the **A** note at the 10th fret of the second string, the middle finger holds the **G** note at the 8th fret of the 2nd string, and the ring finger holds the **E** note at the 9th fret of the 3rd string. (On the record, Eric Clapton bends the 10th fret note of the 2nd string up a tone to a **B** note, then releases the bend to produce an **A** note. To do this smoothly and correctly, you need thin strings and one or two fingers behind the operative finger.)

Lead Riff *(Mark two)*

Here's the lead guitar riff from page 63, but this time with some notes advanced a little to make the rhythm more dynamic:

Dotted notes

Some devices are designed to make writing music easier and quicker. One of these is the dotted note. Instead of two notes tied together, a single note with a dot to its right can be used. The dot increases the length of a note by half its usual length. You've seen the dotted half-note (minim) already – the dot increases its length by half again, so in ⁴4 and ³4 time it lasts for three beats/quarter-notes. Another dotted note you'll often come across is the dotted quarter-note (crotchet) – half the length of a quarter-note is an eighth-note, so the dotted quarter-note lasts for three eighth-notes:

𝅗𝅥. = 1½ half-notes (minims) = 3 quarter-notes time value = 3 beats in ⁴4 and ³4

♩. = 1½ quarter-notes (crochets) = 3 eighth-notes time value = 1½ beats in ⁴4 and ³4

Here are some examples in ⁴4 and ³4 time involving dotted half-notes and dotted quarter-notes:

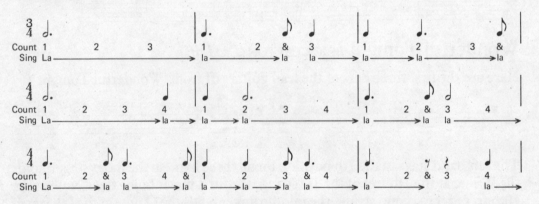

Tap your foot, count the beats, and hum or sing the notes across them as usual. Dotted half-notes are easy to count because they cover three full beats, but dotted quarter-notes in ⁴4 and ³4 time involve half-beats, i.e. coming out or in on the half-beat. In the second bar of the top line above, for example, the dotted quarter-note finishes halfway through the second beat – as your foot reaches its highest point. In the second bar of the bottom line, the dotted quarter-note *starts* on the half-beat and lasts for one and a half beats till the end of the bar.

Some song and instrumental examples with dotted half-notes and dotted quarter-notes are given on the next page.

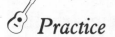

You'll often come across dotted quarter-notes (crotchets) in sheet music, though ties can make the rhythm clearer and easier to follow. On this page there are sections of three songs you've seen already, but here a dotted note replaces each pair of tied notes. I've also included another simple lead riff, this time in **F** major, and a typical bass line for a mid-tempo pop song.

Scarborough Fair TRADITIONAL *(Mark three)*

The Wild Rover TRADITIONAL *(Mark three)*

Jamaica Farewell TRADITIONAL *(Mark two)*

The fourth bar could be written in several different ways. I've given the count for that bar to help you follow it.

Now go back to page 63 and compare the two ways of writing the same thing rhythmically. Then change the ties to dotted notes in 'Danny Boy' and the lead riff on the same page.

Lead riff

Bass Line

Check page 47 for the notes of the bass clef if necessary. Start with the open 6th string **E** note, and remember that the **G** is sharp in the key of **E** major.

The music examples on this page, like every other, are demonstrated on the matching cassette – listen to them to check that what you're playing is correct.

Sixteenth-notes (semiquavers)

Much of today's successful pop music has a 'funky' or 'disco' feel. The main thing these words imply is that the rhythm is based on sixteenth-notes (semi-quavers). Sixteenth-notes have half the time value of eighth-notes (quavers). Dancing music involving sixteenth-notes is always written in ^{4}4 time, and that means it has an underlying stress pattern of four pulses or notes per beat, i.e. sixteen notes per bar of four beats. There are several different ways that you might see sixteenth-notes written. Here are some of the usual ones:

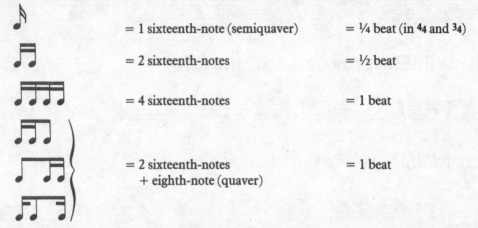

Sixteenth-notes (semiquavers) are often grouped in fours – because four six-teenths add up to one beat, this means each beat will stand out and the rhythm followed more easily. An eighth-note with two sixteenths also add up to one beat, so these will be joined together – the three possibilities are shown above.

Beats and pulses

When the underlying stress pattern of music involves more than two notes per beat, it's probably easier to think of each note in the beat as a 'pulse'. Here's a bar of sixteenth-notes (semiquavers) in ^{4}4 time, shown below a bar of quarter-notes to make the rhythm clear:

Tap your foot on each beat count as always, but this time 'feel' three more pulses after it. You can count '1 a and a, 2 a and a' and so on, or say 'semiquaver' (as shown above), but the main thing is to feel the four pulses or segments of each beat. The examples on the following page should help you to get the feel of sixteenths.

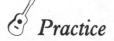

Sixteenth-note strumming pattern

When music has a 'sixteenth feel', the drum part often reflects this with four cymbal (high hat) strikes per beat. The melody and other accompaniment parts will probably involve just *some* sixteenth-notes, but the underlying feel will be four beats and sixteen pulses per bar:

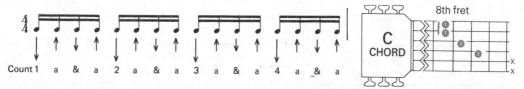

Disco guitar normally means 'partial' chord shapes high up the fretboard, like the **C** chord above. Do sixteen evenly-spaced strums, stressing those on the beat counts (where you tap your foot).

Jive Talkin' BEE GEES (*Strumming pattern*)

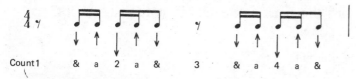

Hold the same high **C** chord shape as above. The eighth-note (quaver) rests cover the first half of the first and third beats, with two strums taking the second half. Guitarists generally do 'air strokes' for the sixteenths they don't sound, (i.e. move the pick up and down but don't hit the strings), or the left hand releases its pressure on the strings just before the pick strikes them – producing a muffled, percussive sound only.

Slow ballads

When a ballad has a very slow pace, there is 'room' in each beat for sixteenth-notes to be put in – 'Hello' and 'I Want To Know What Love Is' for example. Songs like these have full arrangements, but if a solo guitarist accompanied them, this is the sort of pattern he or she could use:

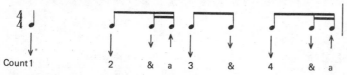

Hold a simple chord like **E** and stress the four strums on the beat counts as before, but keep the tempo slower. Move the right hand down then up, twice for each beat, whether or not you strike the strings, i.e. include air strokes.

Tied sixteenth-notes

Tied notes can be used in music with a sixteenth-note feel, but you'll need to follow the beat and singing indications very carefully:

The sixteenth-note (semiquaver) rest

The sixteenth-note rest looks the same as the eighth-note rest, except that it has two lines on the stem, not one:

    ⅞   eighth-note rest   ⅞   sixteenth-note rest

Here are some examples that include sixteenth-note rests:

If you had difficulties following the patterns above, you can always 'double up' the length of the notes. The last bar with sixteenth-note rests, for example, could be made into two bars for the purpose of following the rhythm more easily:

The dotted eighth-note

The dotted eighth-note lasts half as long again as the eighth-note, i.e. the equivalent of three sixteenth-notes. The first bar of the second line in the examples above involves an eighth-note tied to a sixteenth-note. These tied notes can be written as one – the dotted eighth-note: ♪.

The sixteenth-note may occasionally *precede* the dotted eighth-note: ♪ = ♪.

To improve your feel for sixteenth-note rhythms, here are some segments of bass guitar lines, transcribed from records – play them an octave higher than written. I've also included a 6-string guitar riff in the 'Chic' style.

Layla ERIC CLAPTON *(Bass line)*

The dotted eighth-note lasts for three sixteenths, i.e. ¾ of the beat, with the sixteenth-note taking up the other ¼. This produces a 'jumpy' feel on those beats. Start with the **C** note on the 3rd fret of the 5th string.

Careless Whisper WHAM *(Bass line)*

Rests can be dotted, just like notes. The dotted eighth-note (quaver) means a rest equivalent to three sixteenths. The sixteenth-note following it completes the beat. Mute the string when a rest comes along.

Good Times CHIC *(Bass line)*

This interesting bass line means stopping notes at an eighth or sixteenth length. Double all the time values if you find it hard to follow.

Funk Riff CHIC STYLE *(Lead guitar)*

Summary of notes and rests in ⁴4 and ³4

⁴4 time	Note	Equivalent rest(s)	Beats	Examples
WHOLE-NOTE (SEMIBREVE)	o	▬	4 (Full Bar)	
DOTTED ½ NOTE (MINIM)	𝅗𝅥.	▬ . 𝄽	3	
HALF-NOTE (MINIM)	𝅗𝅥	▬	2	
DOTTED ¼ NOTE (CROTCHET)	𝅘𝅥.	𝄽· (𝄽 𝄾) *or*	1½	
QUARTER-NOTE (CROTCHET)	𝅘𝅥	𝄽	1	
DOTTED ⅛ NOTE (QUAVER)	𝅘𝅥𝅮.	𝄾· (𝄾 𝄿) *or*	¾	
EIGHTH-NOTE QUAVER	𝅘𝅥𝅮	𝄾	½	
SIXTEENTH-NOTE (SEMIQUAVER)	𝅘𝅥𝅯	𝄿	¼	

³4 time	Note	Equivalent rest(s)	Beats	Examples
DOTTED ½ NOTE (MINIM)	𝅗𝅥.	▬	3 (Full Bar)	
HALF-NOTE (MINIM)	𝅗𝅥	𝄽 𝄽	2	
OTHER NOTES	SAME AS IN ⁴4 TIME			SAME AS IN ⁴4 TIME, MINUS ONE BEAT

Note spacing in sheet music

I have deliberately given exact and consistent visual spacing for notes and beats to help you understand rhythm more easily. In each example, one beat is given the same width on the page as another, and each note or rest of the same time value has the same width. The relationship of notes and rests is also maintained visually, i.e. a quarter-note has precisely twice the space of an eighth. In written music the bar length often varies, and the spacing given to notes may not match time values. This is because of the lyrics or number of notes, or the need to limit the number of pages used.

Before looking at less popular rhythms, here are some *rhythm only* segments of well-known melodies in ⁴4 and ³4 time, taken from sheet music or songbooks. Put beat counts beneath the notation, then sing or hum the notes across them. Notice how often singers 'advance' the note from the start of the next bar to the end of the one before. Notice also the old-fashioned way of writing unjoined eighth-notes (quavers) – and the modern way of joining three or four eighth-notes together.

The ₵ time signature (cut time)

Another rhythm you'll come across quite frequently is 'cut time'. This is indicated by the time signature ₵, and is the same as $^2_2$ time:

$$\mathbf{C} \text{ or } \frac{2}{2} = \textbf{Two beats per bar}$$
$$\frac{2}{2} = \textbf{One beat has time value of a half-note (minim)}$$

Two beats per bar and each beat lasting a half-note (minim) means a total time value or length of a bar is the equivalent of two half-notes – or four quarter-notes (crotchets). Thus each bar in ₵ has the same time value as each bar in C or $^4_4$. The difference between the two is that music in cut time is normally played quite fast, with more stress at the halfway point in the bar:

Beats and pulses

When semiquavers were examined on page 68, I suggested you think of them as pulses in each beat. In a similar way, think of the first and third quarter-notes in ₵ time as the beats of the bar (which they are) and tap your foot just on those – as shown above. The second and fourth quarter-notes can be registered as pulses in your mind.

Country music often involves the cut time rhythm, but many pop songs have extra stress in the middle of the bar and are written in ₵ time – like the Beatles' 'I'll Follow The Sun', 'I Will', 'I Wanna Be Your Man', 'I Feel Fine', 'Honey Pie', 'Here, There and Everywhere', 'Help!', 'A Hard Day's Night', 'Get Back', 'Taxman', 'She Loves You', 'Michelle', 'Ob-La-Di Ob-La-Da' and 'Eight Days A Week' for example. Various examples of music written in cut time – classical, traditional and modern, are given on the following page.

Here are segments of well-known songs and instrumentals that are written in cut time. The first two are classical, the next two traditional, and the others – rhythm only – are modern. Remember that the quarter-note speed should be reasonably fast, and stress the first and third quarter-notes.

Moderato SOR

Bourrée BACH

This Train TRADITIONAL

Bill Bailey TRADITIONAL

A Boy Named Sue JOHNNY CASH

And I Love Her BEATLES

Eight Days a Week BEATLES

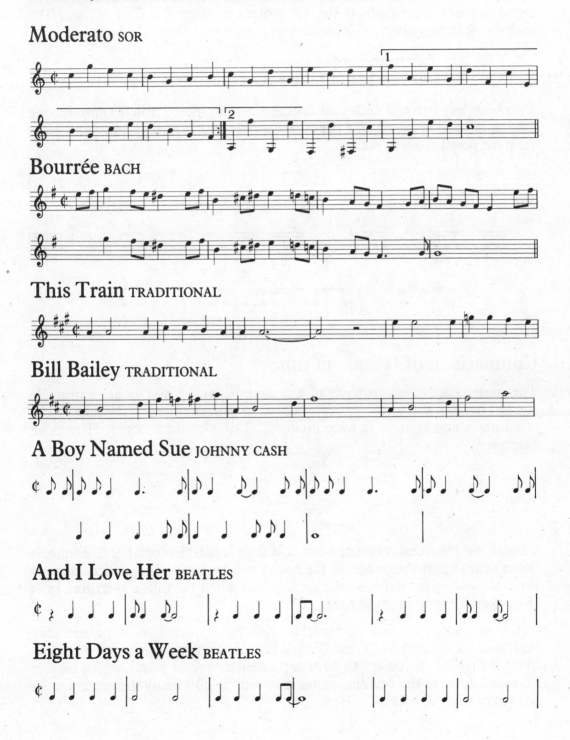

The $^2_4$ time signature

Occasionally you'll come across music written in $^2_4$ time. Generally these will be classical pieces, traditional songs or marches; nearly all modern music found in sheet and songbook form is written in $^4_4$ (or **C**), ¢ or $^3_4$ time. The underlying stress pattern of $^2_4$ means every other beat should be stressed:

> **2 = Two beats per bar**
> **4 = One beat has time value of a quarter-note (crotchet)**

Two beats per bar and each beat lasting a quarter-note (crotchet) produces a total time value or length of a bar of two quarter-notes or the equivalent. Here are some possibilities in $^2_4$ time:

Comparison of $^2_4$ and cut time

The underlying stress patterns of cut time (¢ or $^2_2$) and $^2_4$ are extremely similar, because there are two beats per bar in both rhythms. If the time values of all notes and rests in $^2_4$ were doubled, ¢ time could be used. Here is an example:

Though the total time value of a bar in $^2_4$ time is half that of a bar in ¢ time, it doesn't mean that the tempo of the music will be faster. In practice, there is probably a stronger stress on the second beat when the music is written in $^2_4$ than when it's written in cut time.

You'll appreciate in due course that different transcribers of music may represent the rhythm of the music they hear in slightly different ways. Sometimes it may be customary to write a particular type of music with a certain time signature, or the deciding factor may well be how easily the music can be written or read, or both.

Here are some pieces to give you practice in following and playing music written in ²⁄4 time. The study involves just open string notes and notes on the first three frets.

Study DIABELLI

The Leaving of Liverpool TRADITIONAL

This song can be accompanied with a typical ²⁄4 picking pattern:

T = Right-hand thumb; play bass string
i = Index finger; play 3rd string
r
m } = Middle & ring fingers; play 2nd & 1st strings together

Count 1   &   2   &

Play the chord sequence on to a tape recorder, using the picking pattern above. Then pick out the melody, following the note lengths as accurately as you can.

Drunken Sailor TRADITIONAL

This song has a marching rhythm, with sixteenths coming into some bars.

Jug of Punch TRADITIONAL

Some words of this song are 'jumped' – indicated by the dotted eighth and sixteenth.

The ³8 time signature

³8 time is rarely found in sheet music or songbooks, but sometimes in classical music. The '8' means a beat time value of an eighth-note:

> **3** = **Three beats per bar**
> **8** = **One beat has time value of an eighth-note (quaver)**

Three beats in a bar and each beat lasting an eighth-note (quaver) means a total time value or length of three eighth-notes per bar or the equivalent. Some possibilities in ³8 time are shown below. Notice that the eighth- and sixteenth-notes are usually joined together.

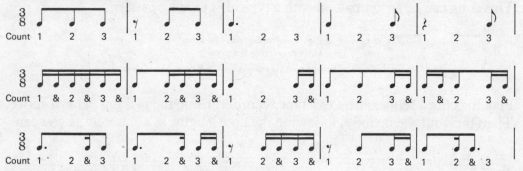

Comparison of ³8 time and ³4 time

The underlying stress patterns of ³8 and ³4 time are similar, because each has three beats in a bar. Doubling the time value of notes and rests in ³8 time might help to make the rhythm clearer – it will also convert the music to ³4 time:

$$\begin{array}{c} \frac{3}{8} \\ \text{Count 1} \end{array} \quad \begin{array}{c} \text{tap} \\ \end{array} \quad \begin{array}{c} \text{2 \& 3} \end{array}$$

Doubling the time values in ³8 produces a bar of ³4 instead, so a natural question to ask is 'Why not write the music in ³4 anyway?' Again, convention plays a part in determining which time signature is used. Modern music is almost never written in ³8 time, whereas some classical music is.

Beats and pulses

I've shown one foot tap for ³8 and three for ³4. Though the speed of music (how fast the beats go by) could in theory be anything from slow to fast whatever the time signature, in practice music in ³8 is played quickly. Tap your foot on the first beat of each bar, and register the other beats as pulses in your mind. Normally music in ³4 time will be played more slowly, but not always.

Play these ³8 pieces briskly, tapping on the first beat of each bar. For practice in writing music, double the note values of 'Greensleeves' and convert it to ³4. ('Greensleeves' and 'Waltz' by Carulli can be found written in both ³8 and ³4).

Study GIULIANI

Waltz CARULLI

Greensleeves TRADITIONAL

The ⁶₈ time signature

The ⁶₈ time signature is sometimes found in more recent music ('The House of the Rising Sun', for example), as well as classical.

> **6 = Six beats per bar**
> **8 = One beat has time value of an eighth-note (quaver)**

A bar with six beats, each lasting an eighth-note (quaver), means a total time value per bar of six eighth-notes. ⁶₈ is a so-called 'compound' rhythm, because the stress pattern produces a natural division of the bar's six beats into two lots of three. The fourth beat is always stressed – though less than the first.

The speed of the beats is fast in ⁶₈ time, so tap your foot only on the first and fourth beats. Think of the first and fourth stressed eighth notes as beats, and the others as pulses which you register in your mind.

Comparison of ⁶₈ time and ³₈ time

A bar in ⁶₈ time is almost the equivalent of two bars in ³₈. The difference is that the fourth eighth-note is stressed *less* than the first in ⁶₈, not *equally* as in ³₈:

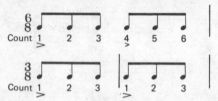

You may see the same piece written in ⁶₈, *and* ³₈. The difference is subtle, and it's often a matter of what writers or players consider the underlying stress pattern to be. 'Greensleeves', for example, has been written in both ways.

Comparison of ⁶₈ time and ³₄ time

Bars in ⁶₈ and ³₄ have the same time value, but different stress points.

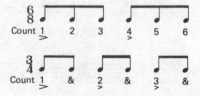

Segments of two classical studies and two traditional tunes written in ⁶₈ time
are given below, followed by the full melody and chord sequence for 'The
House of the Rising Sun'. You may see this song written in ³₄ time as well. I've
included a picking pattern for you to use as an accompaniment to the melody.

Study GIULIANI

Moderato SOR

The Black Velvet Band TRADITIONAL

The Mountains of Mourne TRADITIONAL

The House of the Rising Sun TRADITIONAL

Here is a suitable picking pattern for accompanying this song. Use your thumb
and finger as indicated, or a flatpick. The chords are shown for each bar.

The $^{12}_{8}$ time signature

Occasionally you'll see music written in $^{12}_{8}$ time. This time signature means 12 beats of an eighth-note each:

12 = **Twelve beats per bar**
 8 = **One beat has time value of an eighth-note (quaver)**

12 beats and each one lasting an eighth-note (quaver), means the total time value or length of a bar is twelve eighth-notes or the equivalent. Like $^{6}_{8}$ time, $^{12}_{8}$ is a 'compound' rhythm – it's divided into groups of three eighth-notes. The underlying stress pattern of this rhythm means that the first note of each group of eighths is stressed, with the first of the bar being stressed more than the others as usual:

As with $^{6}_{8}$ time, think of the stress points in each bar as being the beats – four in this case, on counts 1, 4, 7 and 10 – and the other counts as pulses. As shown in the first example above, the first of each group of three eighth-notes is stressed, and that's where you should tap your foot. Make sure that each eighth-note is absolutely equal in length.

Notice the use of the dotted half-note – equivalent to two dotted quarter-notes and two foot taps.

Same song, different time signature

Before researching material for this course, I didn't appreciate how often songs are written with different time signatures. This suggests two things – transcribers obviously have different views on the rhythmic feel or underlying stress pattern of the music, and that the difference between certain time signatures is not great. It's one of emphasis. $^{6}_{8}$ is sometimes written as two bars of $^{3}_{8}$; $^{12}_{8}$ is written as four bars of $^{3}_{8}$ or two bars of $^{6}_{8}$; $^{3}_{8}$ may be written as $^{3}_{4}$, and ₵ could be written as $^{4}_{4}$, to name a few possibilities.

Sometimes music is written in a particular way, or with a particular time signature, to make it easier to write, read or both. One instance is when the $^{12}_{8}$ time signature is replaced by $^{4}_{4}$ – with the use of 'eighth-note triplets'. These are discussed on the next theory page.

The speed of the eighth-notes in $^{12}_8$ time should be reasonably fast.

Little Fugue ZIPOLI

Hold your left hand in the 2nd position, moving temporarily to the 1st position when the **G♯** note comes along. Stress the first of every three eighth-notes.

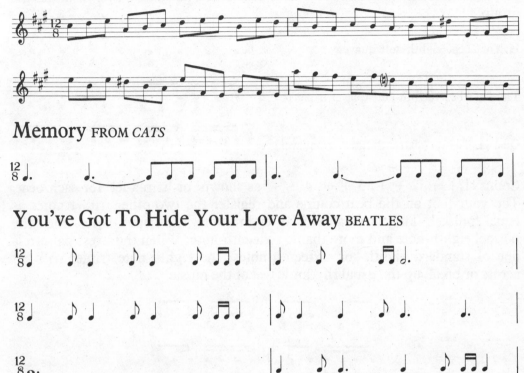

Memory FROM *CATS*

You've Got To Hide Your Love Away BEATLES

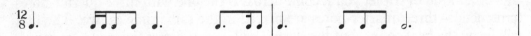

The dotted whole-note is used for a full bar in $^{12}_8$ – equivalent to two dotted half-, four dotted quarter-, or twelve eighth-notes.

Norwegian Wood BEATLES

In one book the time signature for this song is $^3_4$, while in another book it's shown in $^{12}_8$ – something like this:

Notice the use of the dotted half-note rest – equivalent to two foot taps i.e. two dotted quarter-notes or six counts in $^{12}_8$ time.

I'd Rather Go Blind ROD STEWART ET AL

The eighth-note triplet

So far you've seen beats split into halves (two eighth-notes/quavers), or quarters (four sixteenth-notes/semiquavers). Another way a beat can be split is into *three* equal parts – the eighth-note triplet. A triplet means three notes are played in the same time as two. This is indicated by a small 3 over or under the group.

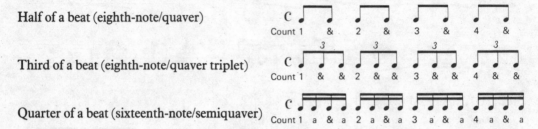

Count '1 + +, 2 + +, 3 + +, 4 + +' as shown, or 'trip-a-let' for each beat. Tap your foot on the beat counts and register the two other triplet notes as equal 'pulses'. The time value of an eighth-note in a triplet is less than the normal eighth-note and more than a sixteenth-note. When the stress pattern is one of standard eighth- or sixteenth-notes, the eighth-note triplet will cut across or break up the usual rhythmic feel of the music:

The effect is a slightly jarring sensation, but if it suits the lyrics and atmosphere of the music it can be exciting and enjoyable. The difference between an eighth-note triplet and two sixteenth-notes and an eighth-note (as in the last example above) can be subtle, but there is a distinct difference.

The quarter-note triplet

The other kind of triplet you'll come across is the one with three quarter-notes (crotchets) – three quarter-notes are played in the same time as two. The first will be on the beat count, but the second will be just *before* the next beat count, and the third just after. Each quarter-note actually has a time value of two-thirds of its usual length. This is used in pop songs to produce a 'push' in the rhythm – used sparingly, it can be effective in providing variety and emphasis. Here is a typical example:

Study GIULIANI

The opportunity to play, 'feel' and compare quarter-notes, eighth-notes, eighth-note triplets and sixteenth-notes is given in one piece.

Baby's in Black BEATLES

This has a fast waltz feel, so it would be better written in $^{12}_8$, where the main rhythmic unit is a dotted quarter-note with the three pulses. Using $^4_4$ means eighth-note triplets occur frequently.

The Fool on the Hill BEATLES

The eighth-note triplets of the melody cut across the straight eighth- and quarter-note feel of the rhythm in this song.

Strawberry Fields BEATLES

In this song there are both eighth-note and quarter-note triplets cutting across the underlying stress pattern.

The swing rhythm

Swing rhythm is called many names – shuffle, swing shuffle, bounce, blues rhythm, boogie-woogie, rhythm and blues, jazz swing, as well as 'swing'. The essential element of music with a swing as opposed to a 'straight' rhythm, is that the second of two notes in a beat is not played halfway through the beat but *nearer the next beat count*. The difference can be shown visually:

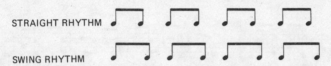

The delay of the second note in a beat produces a 'jumpy' effect – when this happens *throughout* a piece of music it means the underlying stress pattern involves a swing. *Both* melody and accompaniment will normally be swung.

The triplet stress pattern of swing

Whether two or three notes are played per beat, and *whatever the speed* of the music, a swing rhythm means an underlying *triplet* stress pattern:

When there are generally only two notes in each beat – as in many medium paced or faster swing songs – they can be represented by a quarter-note (crochet) and an eighth-note (quaver) with a 3 above, as shown. The quarter-note lasts for two-thirds of the beat, and the eighth-note one-third. To save time, a transcriber may put this sign before the notation: (♫ = ♩♪). This means that eighth-note couplets are written normally, but played with a swing.

Comparison of $\frac{4}{4}$ triplets and $\frac{12}{8}$

Eighth-note triplets in $\frac{4}{4}$ and eighth-notes in $\frac{12}{8}$ are theoretically the same:

Songs with a waltz feel are sometimes written in $\frac{4}{4}$ (i.e. 'Can't Help Falling In Love') when they should be written in $\frac{12}{8}$ (like 'Nights In White Satin'). Bluesy songs – even slow blues like 'I'd Rather Go Blind' – have a swing triplet rather than waltz triplet feel, so should be written in $\frac{4}{4}$.

Swing music is found in most non-classical forms of music. To know whether a song has a swing or straight rhythm can be difficult because sheet music and songbooks often don't indicate a swing rhythm clearly, if at all. 'Shuffle' or 'bounce' is often mentioned rather than swing, and the dotted eighth-note with a sixteenth (♪♬) almost always used in the notation instead of the correct quarter-note and eighth-note with a triplet 3 indication (♩♪).

Wake Me Up Before You Go-Go WHAM

The sheet music of this and the next two songs correctly shows a swing indication before the notation, which means every eighth-note couplet is played with a swing – the first lasts two-thirds of the beat, the second lasts one-third.

Still Crazy After All These Years PAUL SIMON

Yellow Submarine BEATLES

This song is given in a songbook with dotted eighth- notes and sixteenths. The second line shows how the rhythm should be written.

WRONG

RIGHT

To make the transcriber's job easier, the sign ♬ = ♪♪ could be shown above the notation, and normal eighth-note couplets written, as in the songs above.

Songs with a swing rhythm

Here are the titles of various well-known songs that should have a swing in the rhythm – the faster the tempo, the less obvious the swing becomes.

Beatles Songs		Other Songs	
Getting Better	I'm Only Sleeping	This Guy's In Love	Rock Around the Clock
Girl	Maxwell's Silver	Daydream	Blue Suede Shoes
Got to Get You Into My	Hammer	Glory of Love	All Shook Up
Life	Penny Lane	King of the Road	What'd I Say
Help From My Friends	Revolution	Ain't Misbehavin'	Jailhouse Rock
Her Majesty	When I'm Sixty-Four	Scotch & Soda	A Horse With No Name
Honey Pie	Yellow Submarine	Mull of Kintyre	'A' You're Adorable

GUITAR MUSIC NOTATION

Standard notation

When you look round the shops for books of classical instrumental pieces for the guitar, you'll find that the music will almost always be written in standard notation only. Some modern instrumental guitar music is also presented in standard notation on its own – Steve Howe's pieces, Chet Atkins' 'Note-for-note', and John Renbourne's books for example. Occasionally you'll see guitar instruction books which use only standard notation, though most include tablature now – which is examined later in this section.

Two-part notation

So far I've given you only the melody part of songs or instrumentals, or included occasional bass notes which have been joined together with the melody on single stems. The music was kept simple so you could concentrate on reading the pitch of notes and finding them on the fretboard, or counting beats and working out note lengths. You'll find, however, that standard notation for the solo guitarist is almost always written in two separate parts – *both* shown on the same stave, unlike piano music. The stems for the treble notes are drawn upwards, and the bass note stems downwards:

The notes of the bass part will be played by the right hand thumb, and those of the treble by the fingers. Count the parts separately to begin with – each part should add up to the correct time value for every bar. Then work out how the parts fit together rhythmically.

To make two-part notation easier to follow, the same note may be shown as belonging to *both* treble and bass parts. Here is an example:

The two **E** notes and the **G** in the first bar are the melody, and in that capacity they are quarter-notes. In the second bar, the high **B** note (7th fret, 1st string) continues the melody – this dotted half-note lasts for the whole bar. These melody notes are joined to the bass notes, so they become sixteenth-notes in the bass part as well. Examples of two-part notation are given on the opposite page.

Minuet BACH

This piece was given on page 57. The bass part has been included here.

Waltz CARULLI

Study AGUADO

Breezin' RUSS SHIPTON

Standard music notation, unlike tablature, has no signs for guitar embellishments other than the slur line – hence the words describing the particular technique involved. Notice that the last bar of 'Breezin'' has just three quarter-notes' time value – the other beat is the lead-in at the start.

Fingering signs and terms

Classical guitar music often includes fingering indications for the left hand, and sometimes for the right hand where the author or transcriber feels they are necessary. The ones you will probably come across are shown below:

Left-hand fingers

0	= open string (no finger on)	
1	= index finger	normally placed next to note on the stave.
2	= middle finger	
3	= ring finger	
4	= little finger (thumb not used)	

C   = full bar(ree). Index finger presses all six strings down at the same time.

½C   = small bar(ree). Normally index finger presses several strings down at the same time.

TTT or 3P = left hand fingers should be held in 3rd position.

C VI   = full bar at 6th fret.

Right-hand fingers

T	= thumb	normally placed above or below the stave.
i	= index finger	
m	= middle finger	
a	= ring finger	

String indications

① ② ③   1st, 2nd, 3rd string etc. Normally placed below the stave.

Interpretation signs and terms

There are a number of signs and terms used in standard music notation that you need to know. Some indicate the speed the music should be taken or the style in which the music should be played, while others provide information about following the order of the piece. Here are the most common:

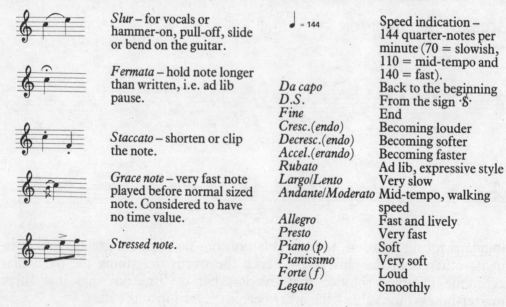

Slur – for vocals or hammer-on, pull-off, slide or bend on the guitar.

Fermata – hold note longer than written, i.e. ad lib pause.

Staccato – shorten or clip the note.

Grace note – very fast note played before normal sized note. Considered to have no time value.

Stressed note.

♩ = 144   Speed indication – 144 quarter-notes per minute (70 = slowish, 110 = mid-tempo and 140 = fast).

Da capo	Back to the beginning
D.S.	From the sign ·𝄋·
Fine	End
Cresc.(endo)	Becoming louder
Decresc.(endo)	Becoming softer
Accel.(erando)	Becoming faster
Rubato	Ad lib, expressive style
Largo/Lento	Very slow
Andante/Moderato	Mid-tempo, walking speed
Allegro	Fast and lively
Presto	Very fast
Piano (p)	Soft
Pianissimo	Very soft
Forte (f)	Loud
Legato	Smoothly

The examples below illustrate the use of some of the finger indications and interpretive signs given on the opposite page. The first and last pieces on this page are in the key of **D** minor, the relative minor key of **F** major – the key of the second piece.

Caprice LEGNANI

mp is short for mezzo piano, i.e. moderately soft. ═══════ means becoming gradually softer. Notice that two notes played together that are next to each other on a line and space are placed either side of the stem for clarity.

Study in F CARCASSI

Antique Waltz RUSS SHIPTON

⟨ means a fast arpeggio across the strings with right hand thumb and three fingers – the action is like tapping your thumb and fingers on a table, one after the other very quickly. It gives the music an olde-worlde traditional effect. ═══════ means becoming gradually louder.

Tablature notation

Tablature is now a popular way of writing guitar music. The essential elements are horizontal lines representing the guitar strings, and numbers on them to show the fret positions of the notes to be played. The underlying chord is indicated above the notation. Sometimes you'll see the fret numbers placed *between* the lines.

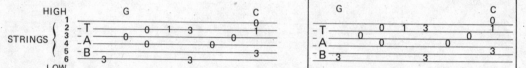

Unitab

Many tablature transcribers use a sort of 'unitab' system that borrows rhythm signs from standard notation. I avoid cluttering the lines by using dots to represent beats.

In the first example above, two notes joined by one line are eighth-notes (quavers), and the note with a line on its own is a quarter-note (crotchet). My system involves evenly spaced beat dots, with notes on the beats played exactly above them. Notes between beats are played exactly halfway unless a swing rhythm is indicated. Where more than two notes come into a beat, the exact lengths of the individual notes is specified below the notation.

Fingering signs

Chord symbols are almost always given with tablature, and together with fret and string positions they can help in choosing the most suitable fingering. When fingering needs to be indicated in tablature, the signs are slightly different from those used in standard notation:

Left hand indications			Right hand indications		
	Thumb	= (t)		Thumb	= T
	First finger	= (i)		First finger	= i
	Second finger	= (ii)		Second finger	= m
	Third finger	= (iii)		Third finger	= r
				Fourth finger	= (iv)

Three types of tablature notation you might come across are used for the pieces below.

Rag in G RUSS SHIPTON

The lines next to the fret numbers show the picking direction – up for fingers, down for thumb.

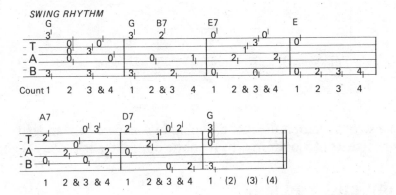

Jesu, Joy of Man's Desiring BACH

This beautiful melody is in $\frac{3}{4}$ time, so each group of three equal notes per beat is an eighth-note (quaver) triplet, as shown in the unitab notation.

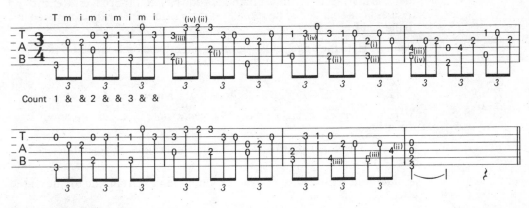

Lead Riff in C RUSS SHIPTON

Three notes come into one beat of the second bar. The first two are sixteenths, the third an eighth – played on the half-beat.

Standard and tablature notation together

Guitar music is now often shown in both tablature and standard notation – in songbooks as well as guitar tuition manuals. The timing of the music is made clearer by the standard notation, while the exact positions of the notes on the fretboard are shown by the tablature. The notes in both notations are shown vertically in line. Here is a segment of a lead guitar part, for example:

When a guitar part is a song accompaniment, the melody is shown in standard notation above – as for 'Streets of London', given on the opposite page.

Guitar embellishments and signs

The guitarist can use a whole array of embellishments. Here are the signs normally used, plus a brief description of each technique:

23 or 02
= *Hammer-on.* The left-hand finger produces a second note which is higher than the first. Here the finger hammers down on to the 3rd fret after the 2nd fret has been sounded. The second example is an open string hammered on to the 2nd fret.

32 or 20
= *Pull-off.* Here the finger pulls the string slightly before coming off to produce a second note lower than the first.

⑧7↑ or ⑧7
= *Bend.* The string is bent up a semitone to the equivalent of the 8th fret.

3⁄5 or 5∖3 = *Slide.* The left-hand finger produces a second note by sliding up or down the string.

10 ∖ or 10∖ = *Slide off.* The finger slides down the string and comes off at an indeterminate fret.

12̃
= *Vibrato.* The left-hand and finger are moved rapidly from side to side on the string.

x9 or 9̇
= *Cut-off* or *damped note.* The string is abruptly stopped from ringing.

⊓
V
= *Right-hand downstroke* } Usually for flatpick.
= *Right-hand upstroke*

∧
= *Right-hand slap.* Normally this means the fingers and heel of the right hand coming down onto all six strings to produce a percussive sound.

12◊
= *Harmonic.* The left hand finger is held directly over the fret wire and just touches the string. It is released quickly when the right hand strikes.

The examples opposite illustrate the use of some of the above signs.

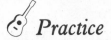
Streets of London RALPH McTELL

The melody 'top line' here is the same as in sheet music, but the other lines are a transcription of the guitar accompaniment (see my notes on page 115).

Lead improvisation RUSS SHIPTON

This improvisation is done over the chords of 'Teach Me Tonight', a jazz blues. The rhythm is swung.

The first bar involves very fast hammer-ons.

Lead Riff RUSS SHIPTON

The string is already bent for the first note in the second bar, then released to the normal 7th fret pitch on the half-beat. The last bar involves a hammer-on and pull-off performed one after the other by the left hand.

WORKING OUT AND TRANSCRIBING MUSIC

Most guitarists have worked out and copied melodies, strum patterns, and riffs, which they've then incorporated into their repertoire. Copying is great for ear training and improving musicianship in general, even though you may find it hard work to begin with. Here is a sequence of steps you can follow when working out and transcribing music from records:

1 **Tape record** the piece you want to transcribe if it's on a single or LP record – tape is much easier to work with.

2 **Tune** your guitar strings to concert pitch using a tuning fork or other instrument that is pitched correctly.

3 **Adjust your 1st string** Choose a high note somewhere on the recording to which you can tune your first string. Check which fret note is the nearest in pitch and then adjust the string slightly to it – you should only be adjusting by less than half a semitone.

4 **Re-tune the other strings** When you're happy that the pitch of the first string matches the recording, tune the other strings to it in the usual way. Now your guitar pitch should be the same as the recording.

5 **Check the underlying stress pattern** Work out the number of bars in a section and the beats in each bar, then put the bar lines and beat indications on music paper.

6 **Find the key and tonic chord** of the music. Listen to the last note of the melody and that should be the key or tonic note. Play the major and minor chords with that note as the root and see which one sounds right.

7 **Find the other chords** Listen to the whole section you're transcribing and experiment with some of the expected chords in the key. Indicate the chords that you discover above the appropriate bars.

8 **Work out the melody notes** Now listen carefully to individual notes of the melody and write down the ones whose pitch and beat place you're sure of – but use a pencil just in case you're wrong!

9 **Fill in** the other notes and chords as you work them out, checking that they sound fine with the recording and seem right for the key.

10 **Guitar parts** When you've sorted out the melody and the chords, the guitar parts (if any) can be looked at. When there's an acoustic guitar accompaniment, check bass runs and hammer-ons to see whether a capo is being used. When working out a lead guitar part, check that the fret and string positions you write down seem right from a fingering viewpoint – if you're unsure of the string being used, choose one and alter it later if needs be.

11 **Rhythm writing** Use tablature to start with, and put beat indications beneath – if your reading and writing of standard notation is weak, put the notes on the stave at your leisure afterwards. Approximate note lengths to the nearest quarter, 8th or 16th – as long as you can reproduce the music accurately enough from what you've written.

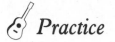

Following written music

Pick a song you know, that you have in written and recorded form. Check that the music is written in the same key as the record, then follow the melody notes, checking chords and the length and pitch of notes while listening to the recording. Do this with several songs until you can relate what you've learnt to what you see and hear. You'll notice that certain approximations are made by transcribers, and you can do the same.

Transcribing melody and guitar part

Now for some hard (but rewarding) work. Choose a song you'd like to play that you haven't got written music for. For a full transcription of melody and guitar part, you'll need two sets of staves and tablature:

Follow the steps given opposite, and transcribe bar lines, beats and tonic chord first. Then write the fret positions on the tablature, on or off the beat. Listen again for the note lengths and write the matching notes on the stave in standard notation – including rests so the bar time values are correct. Add the key signature and other chords – the melody notes might help you to find these. Do the tablature for the guitar part first, then the standard notation.

Transcribing with unitab

You could write the melody only in standard notation, with the guitar part in unitab – as I do when transcribing recorded material or my own.

Working out music – general points

The previous two pages included a sequence of steps to follow when preparing yourself and your guitar for the task of transcribing recorded music. I've put a song on the matching cassette for you to work out and transcribe on to the staves and tablature provided on the opposite page – or you can use them for transcribing another piece of music or song of your choice.

Before trying to work out a melody or guitar part, here are some general points about listening to and working out recorded music which are important to bear in mind:

1 **Left/right balance** Experiment with various settings of the balance on your tape recorder. Different parts may become clearer with the left or right channel higher.

2 **Bass/treble setting** When you've found the right balance setting, try different settings for bass and treble – if you have an equalizer on your tape recorder, this could be very helpful in isolating the particular sound you want to hear.

3 **Slow speed recording** If you have the original recording on an LP or single, and a record player that can be set at a lower speed, you could record the music on to tape at the slow speed. 45rpm down to 33⅓rpm produces a drop of a '4th' or five semitones, while 33⅓rpm down to 16rpm means a drop of an octave. If you're having problems with a very fast phrase, this should help – the notes are lower, but slower. Once you've worked the notes out, adjust the pitch difference carefully.

4 **Copy just a small segment** at a time – a few notes, a bar, or a phrase perhaps. If the phrase is tricky, write down the part of it that you can hear, then fill in the other notes.

5 **A little each day** Like most skills, your ability to work out music from recordings will improve if you do it regularly.

6 **Tackle the difficult phrases first** when you're fresh, and then go on to the easier ones. Take a rest after every fifteen minutes or so, and don't try to do too much in one day.

Transcribing your own music

You can go through exactly the same steps for writing down your own music as those given here for recorded music – except you've got a head start because you know the chords and fret positions for your accompaniment! Put your song or instrumental on tape and transcribe it phrase by phrase as described above.

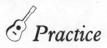

ARRANGING FOR THE GUITAR

Arranging is one of the most difficult tasks for the musician. It requires the skill of composition as well as technical skill. The arranger needs to understand the structure of music in general, as well as the instrument and area of music involved. The best way of understanding how to arrange is to examine and analyse music that has already been arranged.

The guitar comes in various shapes, sizes and types, and is used in different areas of music and in different contexts. This means that arranging for the guitar can mean one of many possibilities:

A Arranging for solo guitar accompanying a vocal melody.
B Arranging for rhythm guitar in a band.
C Arranging for lead guitar in a band.
D Arranging for instrumental solo guitar.
E Arranging for two or more guitars.

The guitar arrangement is required to serve a different function in each of the above situations – involving slightly or greatly different skills and knowledge. This section includes a *brief* summary of the whys and wherefores of arranging guitar parts in the five different contexts.

A/Arranging for solo guitar accompaniment

A solo singer–guitarist requires an arrangement that provides a full and continuous accompaniment for the vocal i.e. a repetitive rhythmic pattern to match the underlying stress pattern of the song. He or she will need to know numerous picking and strumming patterns in various keys, and how to create interest and variety with embellishments, bass runs and semi-melodic additions on the treble strings between the lines and verses. This all involves hard work, taste and judgement as well. Of paramount importance is that the key matches the singer's vocal range – this is where the magical capo can be of great help.

For solo accompaniment then, these are the questions to be answered:

   (i) *The underlying stress pattern* What kind of rhythmic pattern will match the natural stress pattern of the song? Is it waltz or common time; is it a swing or straight rhythm; does it have an eighth-note (quaver) feel, or sixteenth-note (semiquaver) feel; does it have a syncopated, off-beat feel?

   (ii) *Key and chords* Which key suits the singer's vocal range? Are 'open' chords or fretted ones more suitable? Will a capo be necessary and what effect will it have on the sound?

Six main right-hand styles are used for solo guitar accompaniments:

1 The arpeggio style
2 The alternating thumb style
3 The monotonic bass style
4 The slap style
5 The bass strum style
6 The strumming style

} all these styles, patterns and sequences, are demonstrated on the matching cassette.

The most popular patterns in these styles, plus ideas on variations, are given on this and the next few pages. Also provided is a list of songs that are ideal for each particular style or pattern.

1 / The arpeggio style

This style is suitable for ballads, and involves the right-hand thumb and fingers (or flatpick) picking out chord notes one after the other. Here are some typical patterns – written for a common **G** chord with the 3rd fret of the 6th and 1st strings pressed down, and the 2nd fret of the 5th string; the 2nd, 3rd and 4th strings are open. The right-hand thumb should play the notes on the three bass strings, index the 3rd string, middle the 2nd and ring the 1st.

Imagine
Your Song
Michelle
Where Have All the Flowers Gone
Sailing
Candle in the Wind

English Country Garden
The Leaving of Liverpool
Both Sides Now
In My Life
Bright Eyes
Only You

Suzanne
Diamonds and Rust
You've Got a Friend
Jamaica Farewell
If You Could Read My Mind
Another Suitcase in Another Hall

Scarborough Fair
Greensleeves
She's Always a Woman
Black Velvet Band
The Rose of Tralee

Three Times a Lady
Mr Bo Jangles (swing)
Annie's Song
The Queen of Hearts
The Nightingale

Time in a Bottle
House of the Risin' Sun
Plaisir d'Amour
Bird on the Wire
The Wild Rover

For chords other than **G**, play the root note with your thumb at the start of the pattern – the two sequences on the next page illustrate the use of root notes as well giving ideas for variations to the patterns. You could add bass runs, hammer-runs, pull-offs and slides as well as mix patterns.

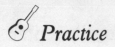

Here are two sequences involving the arpeggio style, in different keys and rhythms. I've included some variations and embellishments, which should give you ideas for adding more interest to the straight patterns.

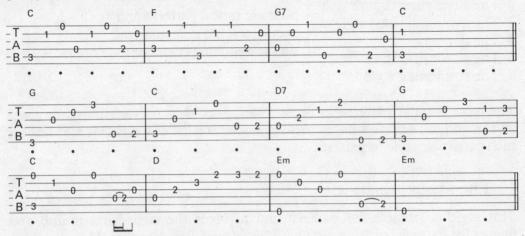

2 / The alternating thumb style

This style is mainly used for modern and traditional folk playing and ragtime but is also suitable for some pop songs. It involves the right-hand thumb striking the root note then another bass note twice over. Here are some popular patterns in this style written for a common G chord:

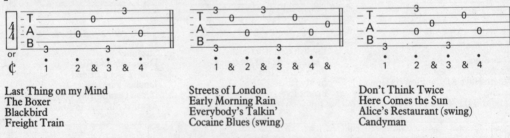

Last Thing on my Mind	Streets of London	Don't Think Twice
The Boxer	Early Morning Rain	Here Comes the Sun
Blackbird	Everybody's Talkin'	Alice's Restaurant (swing)
Freight Train	Cocaine Blues (swing)	Candyman

Here are two sequences with embellishments and variations:

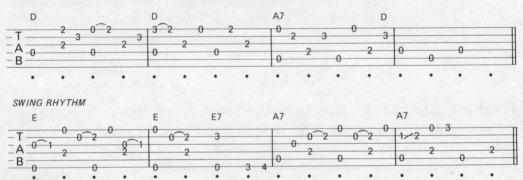

The patterns and sequences are demonstrated on the matching cassette.

3 / The monotonic bass style

The monotonic bass style is mostly used to accompany songs with *swing* rhythms – particularly those in the jazz or blues areas of music. Hold a G chord as before, but swing these patterns.

Trouble in Mind	C. C. Rider	Hallelujah I Love Her So
In the Evening	Dust My Broom	St James Infirmary
Georgia on my Mind	Kansas City Blues	Baby Please Don't Go
Come Back Baby	Stormy Monday Blues	Slip Slidin' Away

The bass notes are often muffled slightly by the heel of the right hand. Here are two sequences in the monotonic bass style (4th string notes *between* beats should be played with the right hand index finger):

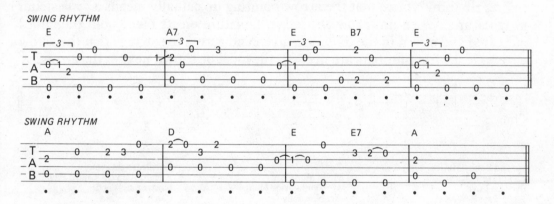

4 / The slap style

This right-hand style involves a percussive slap which emphasizes the 2nd and 4th beats of each bar. The right hand is held lower than usual, near the bridge, and comes down on the strings in a tapping movement – the tips of the fingers on the treble strings and the heel of the hand on the bass.

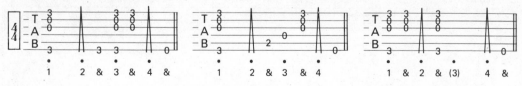

Don't Give Up On Us	Moondance (swing)	Save The Last Dance For Me
You're So Vain	Till There Was You	Under the Boardwalk
May You Never	Don't It Make My Brown Eyes	You Are The Sunshine of My Life
I Can See Clearly Now	Blue (swing)	Sunny
Do That To Me One More Time	Baker Street	And I Love Her

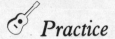
Here are two sequences with variations to the usual patterns and chords:

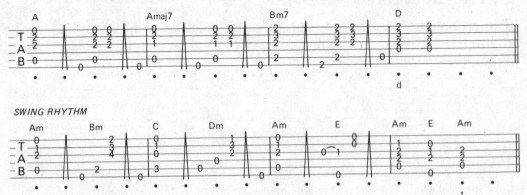

5 / The bass-strum style

This style is particularly suitable for accompanying country-flavoured songs in cut time, though it can be used for faster pop songs that require a steady, rolling rhythm. Notice that the arrow pointing up actually means a *down*strum in tablature. When an arrow is used in tablature on its own, hold the chord indicated and strum in the direction given and across the strings that the arrow covers. If the fret numbers are needed, they will be shown next to the arrow.

Me and Bobby McGee
City of New Orleans
Bye Bye Love
Eight Days A Week
I Walk the Line

Rave On
Hello Mary Lou
Mr Tambourine Man
Act Naturally
Help!

Lucille (slight swing)
A Hard Rain's A-Gonna Fall
Norwegian Wood
Catch The Wind
Take It To The Limit (Swing)

6 / The Strumming style

Some of the rock orientated strumming patterns are given here, though additional patterns and variations to these when played in the context of a band are shown on page 107. Strumming patterns for the solo guitarist need to be full in order to keep the rhythm going behind the vocalist. Here are a variety of patterns that will suit different kinds of rhythms and types of music:

BALLAD

Rhinestone Cowboy
If I Said You Have a Beautiful Body
It Never Rains in Southern California
Leaving on a Jet Plane

FOLK ROCK

Lyin' Eyes
My Sweet Lord
Take It Easy
Year of the Cat

ROCK

I Only Want to be With You
Kids in America
Pretty Vacant
Regatta de Blanc

BOOGIE

Rockin' All Over The World
Get Back
I Can Help (swing)
Caroline
No Particular Place to Go (swing)

SWING POP (use bar chord)

Don't Stop
Yellow Submarine
Raindrops Keep Falling On My Head
Mellow Yellow
Sunny Afternoon

ROCK BACKBEAT (use bar chord)

It's Only Rock'n'Roll
Proud Mary
The Word
You Can't Do That
One Of These Nights

SLOW POP BALLAD

Let It Be
Hey Jude
Bridge Over Troubled Water
Father and Son

FUNK

Listen to the Music
Night Fever
Pinball Wizard
Layla

WALTZ

Masters of War
Mull of Kintyre (swing)
Morning Has Broken
You've Got to Hide Your Love Away

The boogie pattern involves adding the sixth note of the chord on the 2nd and 4th beats (**E** in the case of the **G** chord). Experiment with adding notes to the standard chord shapes, and fitting in bass runs, hammer-ons and slides, as well as varying the patterns. Try the occasional rhythm stop too – often at the start of a verse or chorus.

B/Arranging for rhythm guitar in a band

The rhythm guitarist in a band should listen to the patterns the drummer and bass guitarist have chosen, and either play along or work off them, filling in the gaps. Being only part of the overall rhythm and sound, the rhythm guitarist has more freedom than the solo player – he or she can strum a continuous and repetitive pattern, or do 'chops' (damped chordal downstrums) here and there, without the risk of being boring or too spacey. Whatever the rhythm player chooses to do, he or she must know movable chord shapes – which normally involve a bar. Here are the most important ones:

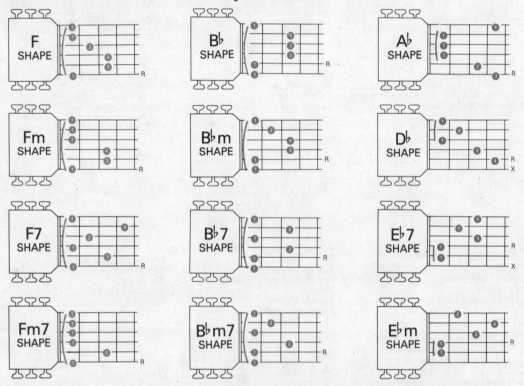

The root note of each shape is indicated (R) next to the appropriate string. Wherever the chord shape is on the fretboard, it will remain the same type of chord, i.e. major or minor or 7th, and the note on the same string will be the one that gives the chord its name. All movable shapes can be broken down into a number of partial chord shapes, like the **F** shape, for example:

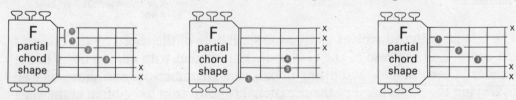

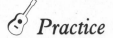
Transposing

The rhythm guitarist can transpose from key to key by shifting moveable chord shapes up and down the fretboard. Play the three main chords in the key of G major, for example:

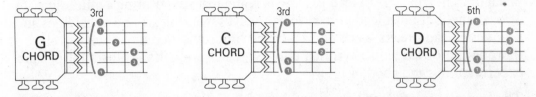

These shapes moved up two frets become the chords **A**, **D** and **E** in the key of **A** major; two frets down they become **F**, **B**♭ and **C** in **F** major, and so on. A useful exercise would be for you to play all the scale chords, major and minor, for the five popular guitar keys – see page 39 – using *only* movable shapes.

Rhythm patterns for the electric guitar

When playing continuous rhythm patterns, the electric guitarist normally uses the middle pick-up position to activate both pick-ups, and turns the treble down slightly. For the chunky, attacking heavy rock sound, the volume will be turned up too! The disco and reggae patterns require a shriller sound – partial chord shapes high on the fretboard, with the treble up. Because the drummer and bass guitarist provide the rhythmic 'backbone' of a band, the guitarist is free to syncopate much more than the solo player – as shown by these examples of rock and pop rhythms (all notes should be strummed):

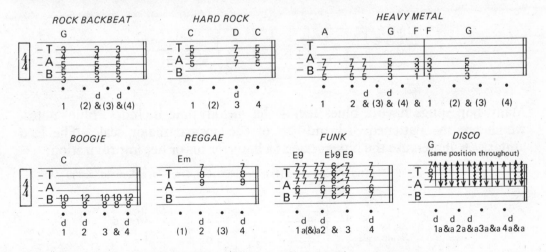

The rhythm guitarist in a band will do a lot of damping (d) and muffling(↑) of strings and notes in most areas of music.

C/Arranging for lead guitar in a band

When a lead guitarist like Duane Eddy or Hank Marvin plays the melody of an instrumental piece which has been arranged for a band, it is mainly a question of choosing where to play the melody notes on the fretboard and what effects pedal to use. This type of lead playing is really just substituting a guitar line for a vocal line, but most lead guitar work involves working around vocal lines and producing lead breaks – and this so-called 'improvisational' playing involves a thorough knowledge of rhythms, chords, scales and riffs – plus a lot of hard experimenting and good taste!

The lead player needs to have a number of movable scales under his fingertips. Most lead work in popular music is based on either the major pentatonic scale or the blues pentatonic scale. The first consists of notes taken from the normal major scale – in the key of **C** major these major pentatonic scale patterns are the kind used by lead players:

The C major pentatonic scale (1st, 2nd, 3rd, 5th & 6th of C major scale)

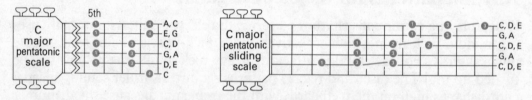

The circled numbers indicate the left-hand fingers, and the notes produced are given next to the strings. The patterns can be moved up or down the fretboard for other keys. Occasionally the 'open', non-movable pattern may be used:

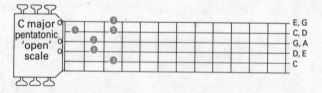

Many pop songs have a blues feel – the melody line includes 'blue' notes, which are the flattened 3rd and 7th of the normal major scale. The lead guitarist will then use the blues scale as a basis for his or her improvization:

The C blues scale (1st, ♭3rd, 4th, ♭5th, 5th, ♭7th of C major scale)

The movable blues scale is like the major pentatonic scale moved three frets up – plus the flattened 5th note.

Interesting lead lines include hammer-ons, pull-offs, slides and bends, stopped notes, double notes, occasional chords, as well as variations in attack and speed. The two guitar breaks below include some of the possibilities:

D/Arranging for instrumental solo guitar

The solo instrumentalist must play *both* melody line and accompaniment, as well as hold down the rhythm. The area and style of music, as well as fretboard fingering possibilities in different keys, will determine exactly how the music is arranged.

Jazz instrumental music

Non-classical forms of guitar music tend to be chord based. Jazz players use movable jazz chord shapes – the highest note of the chord will be the melody note, though occasional melody notes will be played on their own. Here are some common shapes – these are all 'movable' if the strings not fretted are muted.

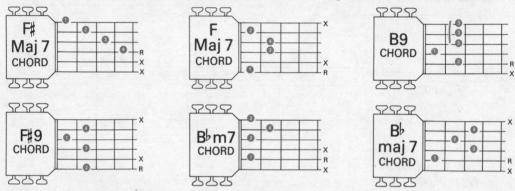

Blues instrumental music

In blues music, dominant 7th chords are often used i.e. A7, D7 and E7 in A major. Partial chord shapes are often fingered:

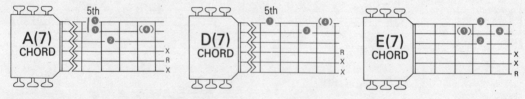

Flamenco instrumental music

Flamenco guitar music is much more concerned with rhythm than melody, and consists largely of strummed chords and arpeggios of chords. Two distinctive facets of flamenco music are the use of the out-of-key major chord one semitone above the tonic, and the frequency of minor keys.

Classical instrumental music

Like flamenco music, most classical guitar music is instrumental, but it is very melody orientated. The melody is often harmonized in a horizontal way rather than only vertically, i.e. the bass part is a counter melody or has a distinctive movement of its own. The general idea when putting together a classical guitar arrangement is to be very structured, with the bass and harmony lines moving gently, i.e. no large jumps in pitch.

In the waltz jazz sequence below, the chords can be strummed or plucked. The blues ragtime should *not* be swung – use your right-hand thumb for the beat notes. You saw the Bach piece before on page 75 – this time the bass part is included. Can you work out the underlying chords?

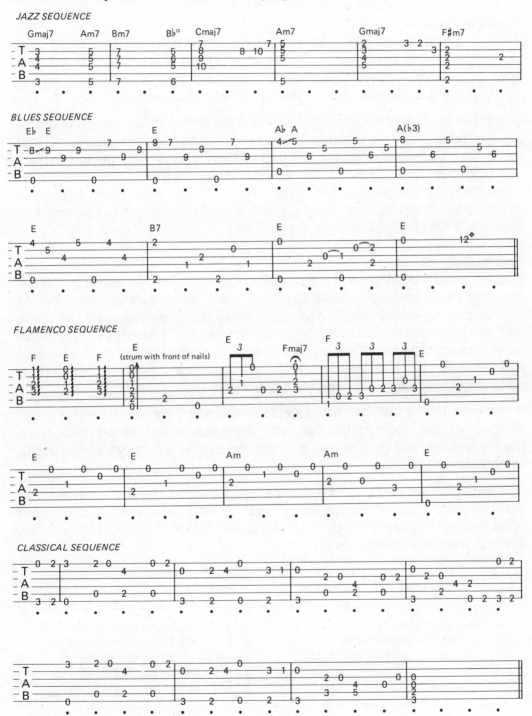

E/Arranging for two or more guitars

Like solo instrumental guitar arrangements, the parts taken by two or more players will vary according to the type of music involved.

Classical music

Classical guitar duets, like solo arrangements, are carefully structured both harmonically and rhythmically. The two parts need to work off and complement each other – interesting harmony lines and different rhythm patterns should make the total sound more than the sum of the two parts.

One guitar may play the treble part only and the other the bass; both parts may involve treble and bass to produce a very full harmony; sometimes 'call and answer' sequences between the two guitars can be used. One obvious advantage of having more than one guitar needs to be explored – the fact that an agreeable combination of notes that can't be produced by one player because of limitations in fingering, may be produced by two. An example of classical duet music in $^6_8$ time is given on the opposite page.

Folk/blues/rock/jazz

In these non-classical areas of music a duet arrangement will normally consist of one guitar providing a steady rhythm – often with a repetitive strumming rhythm pattern – while the second guitar picks out single notes, i.e. plays the lead part. In acoustic folk and blues music, there could be two rhythm guitar parts working off each other (one picking, one strumming, or both picking); each playing different patterns with different stress points, plus a third guitarist playing the melody as shown opposite.

When two jazz guitarists play together, one will play steady and slightly damped strums, four to the bar, and the other will take the melody or improvisational lead part, working round the regular strums with a variety of rhythmic syncopations.

Jazz arrangements often involve altered and extended chords, so rather than use a 'blanket' scale for playing lead against all the chords (as the pop guitarist often does – see page 108), the jazz player will follow the chords closely and alter the scale he uses accordingly:

Chord type (over which scale can be played)	Scale
Major 7ths and major 9ths	1 2 3 4 5 6 7 (normal major scale)
Minor, minor 7ths and minor 9ths	1 2 ♭3 4 5 ♭6 ♭7 (natural minor scale)
Dominant 7ths, 9ths, 11ths and 13ths	1 2 3 4 5 6 ♭7 (mixolydian mode)
Augmented	1 2 3 ♭5 ♯5 ♭7 (whole tone scale)
Diminished 7th	1 2 ♭3 4 ♭5 ♯5 6 7 (diminished scale)

In the folk sequence below, guitar two has a capo on the 5th fret. Guitar three plays lead based on the sliding C pentatonic scale given on page 108. The jazz sequence is typically chromatic (semitone by semitone). Try writing these sequences in standard notation.

NOCTURNE DE SALON (CARULLI)

MODERN FOLK SEQUENCE

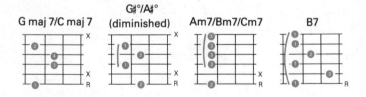

JAZZ SEQUENCE

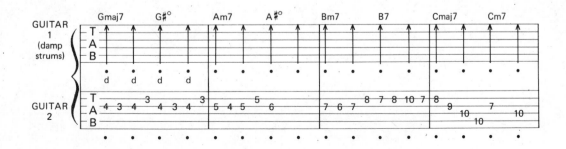

SHEET MUSIC EXAMPLES

This section of the book provides segments taken from the original sheet music of popular songs, which are analysed from both theoretical and practical points of view. This should help you to get the most out of the music you buy, and in a sense will summarize the information that has been given in this course. In case you're unsure about any of the analytical points made, there are page references for you to refer to the relevant section of the book.

Streets of London
RALPH McTELL

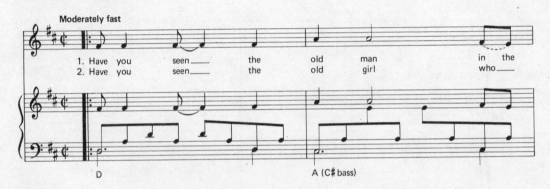

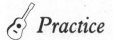

General Three staves are joined at the start of each line of music. The top line is the melody, the lower two the keyboard accompaniment – middle stave (treble clef) for right hand notes, lowest stave (bass clef) for the left. Notes vertically in line are played together. [See pages 8–18 and 88–90]

Pitch The two sharp signs (♯) at the start of each stave means all **F** and **C** notes are sharpened (played one semitone higher). The last note of the melody (not shown here) normally indicates the tonic note of a song, and later in the sheet music it is shown as a **D**. Two sharps in the key signature, a **D** major chord for the first bar of the verse, and the last note a **D** means the music is written in the key of **D** major. The 'expected' notes to be included in both melody and accompaniment are therefore: **D, E, F♯, G, A, B,** and **C♯**. The expected chords built on and from those notes are: **D** major, **Em, F♯m, G** major, **A** major and **Bm**. Sometimes the lowest note of a chord may not be the root, as in **A** (**C♯** bass). Normally this is written **A/C♯**. There are no accidentals, i.e. ♯, ♭ or ♮ next to a note, so the arrangement stays in key for these four bars. There is a temporary key change later when the **E7** chord is used. Here is the full chord sequence, as given in the sheet music (one chord symbol per bar except where indicated):

McTell uses this shape (2nd fret capo)

Verse	**D**	**A/C♯**	**Bm**	**F♯m/A**	**G**	**D/F♯**	**E₇**	**A13★**	
	D	**A/C♯**	**Bm**	**F♯m/A**	**G**	**D/F♯**	**A₇**	**D**	**D**
Chorus	**G**	**D**	**D/F♯ & A₇**	**B & Bm₇/A**	**E₇/G♯**	**A₇**	**A₇**		
			2 BEATS EACH	2 BEATS EACH					

(The second line of the chorus is the same as the second verse line)

(See pages 20–47)

Rhythm The time signature ₵ means $^2_2$ or cut time. In practice, this is a moderately fast or fast tempo with extra stress on the third beat of each bar. Some syncopation occurs in the melody, with words stopping and starting between beats – making the vocal line more interesting – but the bass line is a steady arpeggio type of accompaniment. The right-hand part follows the melody but includes two higher pitched notes that are joined to the bass part. Each part adds up to the equivalent of four quarter notes per bar, and they are written the way they are to make reading the music easier. The small notes and the dotted slur lines apply to the words of the second verse. [See pages 48–87.]

Arranging for the guitar

Sheet music arrangements are designed by and for keyboard players, and therefore guitarists must examine them carefully. For instance, Ralph McTell actually uses the **C** chord shape (and related shapes) which is transposed to the key of **D** by his capo being on the 2nd fret. Also, the right-hand style he uses is alternating thumb – as shown on page 95 – and not the arpeggio style given in the sheet music. Apart from significant variations like these, many accompaniment notes will be different, or in a different order from the record. Another difference between the recorded and written music here is the 'A bass' given for the **F♯m** chord. This transposes to a **G** bass for the **Em** chord, but Ralph McTell plays the usual **E** bass note, not **G**. [See pages 100–113.]

Wonderful Tonight

ERIC CLAPTON

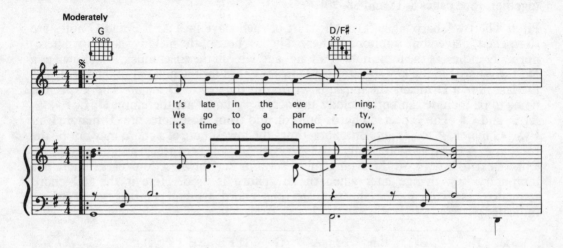

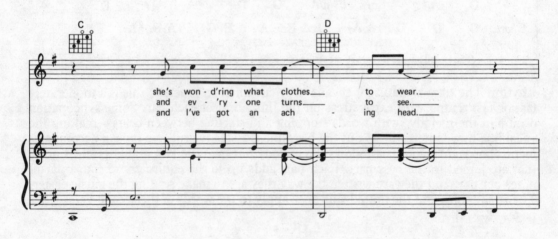

General The lower two staves are bracketed because they are the accompaniment to the melody in the top line. The bar lines are normally drawn right across the lower two staves. Moderately means ♩=108–120 in classical terms, i.e. moderato =108–120 quarter-notes/beats per minute. The double line with two dots in front means (in conjunction with a similar sign further on) the section is repeated. In fact it's played three times through for the verses. 'D.S.' refers the reader back to the sign ·𝕾· after another section has been played. Another common sign is the coda or ending sign: ⊕. This is used in the sheet music for 'Wonderful Tonight', together with 'D.S. '𝕾' al Coda ⊕', which directs you to repeat the music from the '𝕾' sign on to the ending from the coda sign. See pages 8–18 and 88–90.

Pitch One sharp sign, a **G** chord at the start, together with a **G** note to end the melody means the key of **G** major. Thus the 'expected' notes are: **G, A, B, C, D, E,** and **F♯**, and the expected chords are **G** major, **Am, Bm, C** major, **D** major and **Em**, or perhaps the extended versions of those chords. In fact the three main chords are used in the four bars given on the opposite page. In this case, diagrams have been given for the chords, not just the names. These are shown with the nut at the top. Also – and this is the exception rather than the rule – the diagrams probably show the fingerings used on the recording. No accidentals here means the music remains 'in key', as it does throughout. Here is the full chord sequence:

Verse **G**	**D/F♯**	**C**	**D**	**G**	**D/F♯**	**C**	**D**		
C	**D**	**G & D/F♯**	**Em**	**C**	**D**	**G**	**D/F♯**	**C**	**D**
		(2 BEATS EACH)							
Chorus **G**	**C**	**D**	**G & D/F♯**	**Em**	**C**	**D**	**C**	**D**	**G**
			(2 BEATS EACH)						

(See pages 20–47)

Rhythm The time signature $^4_4$ means there are four beats of a quarter-note each per bar. Thus each part must add up to the equivalent of four quarter-notes for every bar. Notice that *both* right- and left-hand parts are split into two sometimes. This is to show clearly how long the different notes last in the recording. There is the usual syncopation in the vocal line for interest, but otherwise the rhythm is steady and involves nothing unusual. [See pages 48–87.]

Arranging for the guitar
The solo guitarist accompanying a vocal line can use an arpeggio style pattern for this ballad, plus perhaps some bass runs – which could be taken directly from the bass guitar part, transcribed in the sheet music. Strumming would probably be a little boring at a slow tempo, and maybe too 'heavy', and the other styles too strong on each of the beats. With some ingenuity, the haunting lead guitar riff can be squeezed into an arpeggio pattern:

(See pages 100–113)

Sultans of swing
MARK KNOPFLER

Med. Bright Rock

1. You get a shiv-er in the dark, it's rain-ing in the park, but mean-
2. step in-side but you don't see too ma-ny fa-

- time,
- ces

General Like the previous examples, the introduction to the song has been omitted.

'Med. Bright Rock' means a reasonably dynamic and punchy sound at a moderate tempo. The '𝄋' sign is used again here – for the repeat of the verse sequence. The letters *mf* stand for *mezzo-forte*, i.e. reasonably loud. [See pages 8–18 and 88–90.]

Pitch The key signature means the key of **F** major or its relative minor key **D** minor – both involve one flat note, **B**♭. Because the song starts and ends with a **Dm** chord, that's probably enough to decide that the song is in a minor key, but the last note of the melody is in fact a **D**. Thus the 'expected' notes here are **D, E, F, G, A, B**♭ and **C**, though sometimes the 6th and 7th notes of the scale might be sharpened, i.e. **B** natural and **C**♯ could occur. Bars three and four do have a **C**♯ in the accompaniment – **C**♯ is part of the dominant **A7** chord. The expected chords in the key of **D** minor are: **Dm, F** major, **Gm, Am, B**♭ major and **C** major. The dominant 7th chord is often borrowed from the major key with the same tonic note, so in a sense the **A7** chord is expected in **D** minor. Here is the chord sequence:

Dm	C & B♭ (2 BEATS EACH)	A₇	A₇	Dm	C & B♭ (2 BEATS EACH)	A₇	A₇
F	F	C	C	B♭	B♭	Dm	Dm & B♭ (2 BEATS EACH)	C	C

[See pages 20–47]

Rhythm The time signature means four beats and four quarter-notes per bar. The small notes in the first two bars apply to the second verse lyrics. The bass part is taken directly from the bass guitarist with its steady mid-tempo pop pattern of dotted quarter note plus 8th, while the melody above is quite straight. [See pages 48–87.]

Arranging for the guitar
A guitarist in a band can follow Mark Knopfler's playing, and rely on others to fill in the rhythm gaps. Knopfler does some chordal work while singing, then lead riffs between vocal lines. Where there are two six-string guitarists in a band, one could play a continuous rhythm pattern throughout, while the other could concentrate on lead. The bass guitar pattern used for this song will mean the slap style should work well for the solo or duo situation. You could use the open chords given in the sheet music, but they aren't as effective as shapes higher up the fretboard. The problem is to play the chords that Knopfler does, but to include the bass root notes as well. He fingers partial chord shapes like this (shown in sheet music style):

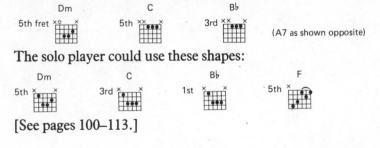

The solo player could use these shapes:

[See pages 100–113.]

Nights in white satin

JUSTIN HAYWARD

General The sign just above the notation indicates the overall speed of the music – the dotted quarter note is the basic unit of rhythm, i.e. when each foot tap comes. Thus 56 foot taps should occur in the space of one minute, which means a slow tempo. [See pages 8–18 and 88–90.]

Pitch The key signature of one sharp means all **F** notes are played sharp unless a natural sign is placed next to them – as in the fourth bar shown. All **F** notes in this bar should be played natural because an accidental sign affects the same notes that follow in the same bar. The last note of the melody is an **E**, so together with the chords indicated and the melody notes, this means the key of the music is **E** minor, and not the relative **G** major. Thus the expected notes are **E, F♯, G, A, B, C** and **D**, and chords of **Em**, (rarely **F♯♭5**), **G** major, **Am, Bm** (or **B**), **C** major and **D** major. The **F** chord is therefore an out-of-key chord used to create more interest, as is the **A** major chord which occurs later. The full chord sequence is:

Em & D	Em & D	C & G	F & Em	Em & D	Em & D	C & G	F & Em
A	C	Em & D	Em & D	A and C chords last one bar each.			
				The others last half a bar each.			

[See pages 20–47.]

Rhythm The time signature means the total time value of one bar is twelve eighth-notes or the equivalent. You'll notice dotted quarter-notes, dotted quarter-note rests and eighth-notes joined in threes. The underlying stress pattern involves a stressed eighth-note every three – usual for compound time. In $^{12}_8$ time it's easier to think of each bar as having four beats with three small pulses per beat, i.e. ♫♩♫♩♫♩♫♩. Thus the dotted quarter-note lasts for one beat or foot tap and the dotted half-note for two. The group of six sixteenth-notes (semiquavers) are played in the time of one foot tap, with the pulses on the 1st, 3rd and 5th notes. The dotted sixteenth-note in the short lead-in lasts for three thirty-second notes (demi-semiquavers) and is joined to a thirty-second note. The thirty-second note is indicated by three lines on the stem and is half the time value of a sixteenth note – these are rarely seen in today's sheet music. The 2° sign means '2nd time', i.e. for the second verse, and refers to the small notes. [See pages 48–87.]

Arranging for the guitar

$^{12}_8$ time can be treated like four bars of $^3_8$ or $^3_4$, with more emphasis on the 1st, 4th, 7th and 10th eighth-notes. A strum pattern is probably more appropriate than a picking one for this song, because it has more bite and the eighth-notes can be played more quickly. Use a strum pattern with downstrums on each eighth-note or pulse – they should be very short and quickly played (if 56 dotted quarter-notes are to be covered in a minute, that means 3×56 downstrums.) Occasional, very quick and even shorter upstrums may be included:

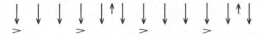

Emphasize the first strum more than the others. If the melody is too low for the singer, use a capo or transpose the music and chords to another key. [See pages 100–113.]

APPENDIX 1 – PITCH

Intervals

When analysing harmonies, musicians refer to particular intervals of pitch between notes, like '3rds' and '5ths' for example. Pitch intervals are listed below.

NO. OF SEMITONES	INTERVAL	EXAMPLE	
0	Perfect prime (unison notes)	C – C	
1	Augmented prime	C – C♯	enharmonically
1	Minor 2nd	C – D♭	equal intervals
2	Major 2nd	C – D	
3	Augmented 2nd	C – D♯	
3	Minor 3rd	C – E♭	,,
4	Major 3rd	C – E	
5	Perfect 4th	C – F	
6	Augmented 4th	C – F♯	
6	Diminished 5th	C – G♭	,,
7	Perfect 5th	C – G	
8	Augmented 5th	C – G♯	
8	Minor 6th	C – A♭	,,
9	Major 6th	C – A	
10	Augmented 6th	C – A♯	
10	Minor 7th	C – B♭	,,
11	Major 7th	C – B	
12	Octave	C – C′	

Note: Intervals over an octave are called major or minor 9ths, 10ths etc.

Chords

When analysing a chord, the notes are related to the major scale of the root note:

CHORD TYPE	CHORD	NOTES IN CHORD						EXAMPLE CHORD	NOTES IN CHORD					
Major	Major	1	3	5				A	A	C♯	E			
	Major 6th	1	3	5	6			A6	A	C♯	E	F♯		
	Major 7th	1	3	5	7			Amaj7	A	C♯	E	G♯		
	Major 9th	1	3	5	7	9		Amaj9	A	C♯	E	G♯	B	
	Major 6/9	1	3	5	6	9		A6/9	A	C♯	E	F♯	B	
Dominant	Dom. Major	1	3	5				A	A	C♯	E			
	Dom. 7th	1	3	5	♭7			A7	A	C♯	E	G		
	Dom. 9th	1	3	5	♭7	9		A9	A	C♯	E	G	B	
	Dom. 11th	1	3	5	♭7	9	11	A11	A	C♯	E	G	B	D
	Dom. 13th	1	3	5	♭7	9	11 13	A13	A	C♯	E	G	B	D F♯
Minor	Minor	1	♭3	5				Am	A	C	E			
	Minor 6th	1	♭3	5	6			Am6	A	C	E	F♯		
	Minor 7th	1	♭3	5	♭7			Am7	A	C	E	G		
	Minor 9th	1	♭3	5	♭7	9		Am9	A	C	E	G	B	
	Minor 7th ♭6	1	♭3	♭5	♭7			Am7 ♭5	A	C	E♭	G		
Other	Diminished 7th	1	♭3	♭5	♭♭7			A dim.7	A	C	E	G♭♭ (=F)		
	Augmented	1	3	♯5				A aug.	A	C♯	E♯ (=F)			
	Sustained 4th	1	4	5				A sus.	A	D	E			

The m7♭5 chord is in key if its root is the seventh note of the tonic major scale. If **B♭** major is the key of the music, for example, the **Am7♭5** chord is the expected 7th chord. The diminished and augmented chords are out-of-key chords – in any key. They are used as passing chords. The diminished chord is similar to the dominant 7th chord and can sometimes be used as a substitute for it.

Transposing

Transposing means changing music from one key to another. All melody and accompaniment notes must go up or down by the same number of semitones. Once you can remember which notes and chords are expected in which keys, transposition naturally becomes easier. To start with it helps to understand intervals – shown opposite. Say you have a set of chords in the key of **A** major, for example, **A**, **D** and **E**, and you want to go up in pitch a little to suit the singer's voice. You could try changing the pitch to **B♭** or **C**. For **B♭**, the rise is just one semitone. That can be calculated quite easily. A change from **A** to **C** means a rise of three semitones. You could think of this as a rise of a minor 3rd and count up from the original note or chord to the new one in letters first, then check that the interval is a minor 3rd:

A	tone	B	s/tone	C		A	B	C	D	E
1		2		3		1	2	3	4	5
		up a minor 3rd		↑				up a perfect 5th		↑

When the change in pitch is greater, you should always transpose with intervals in mind – this would save you counting up semitone by semitone. Going from **A** to **E**, for example, is going up by a 5th. All notes and chords can be calculated quite quickly in the way shown above. The 'colour' of each chord must remain the same (minor stays a minor, 7th stays 7th, and so on). If notes are accidentals, then you need to be careful calculating your intervals – the note must still be an accidental in the new key.

Transposing instruments

Some instruments play music that's written in one key but the *actual* pitch is in another key. The **B♭** clarinet, for example, when playing music written in the key of **C**, is actually playing in the key of **B♭**. This is usually done to make the music easier to read. Some instruments play in the same key as the music is written, but sound an octave below or above – guitar music, for example, sounds an octave lower than it is actually written. When the keyboard player plays middle **C**, the note will sound an octave higher than the 'middle **C**' of the guitarist. This is because guitar music is written on the treble clef, not the bass clef, by convention.

Enharmonic notes

A♭ is the same pitch as **B♭**, **C♯** is the same pitch as **D♭**, and so on. These are enharmonic notes, i.e. equal in pitch. In the rarely used keys, **C♭**, **F♭**, **B♯** and **E♯** are also used – these notes are played as **B**, **E**, **C** and **F** respectively. In the very obscure keys double sharps (♯♯) and double flats (♭♭) may be used. These notes are altered by a tone, i.e. **D♭♭** is played as **C**, and **D♯♯** as **E**.

Major scale degrees

The major scale steps or degrees are distinguished by roman numerals. They are also given names to indicate their relationship to the tonic note. These names are used for harmonic analysis. ('Tetrachord' refers to four notes of a scale with two tones and a semitone interval between them. These 'half-scales' can be combined to produce other major scales.)

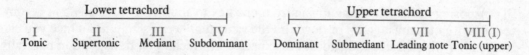

Lower tetrachord				Upper tetrachord			
I	II	III	IV	V	VI	VII	VIII (I)
Tonic	Supertonic	Mediant	Subdominant	Dominant	Submediant	Leading note	Tonic (upper)

Natural, harmonic and melodic minor scales

The natural minor scale has the same notes as its relative major, i.e. **C** major and **A** minor. For purposes of harmony, the seventh note was raised a semitone, which is included in the harmonic minor scale. The tone-and-a-half interval between the sixth and seventh scale steps was then considered too great, and the sixth note was raised by a semitone – but only when the pitch is rising. This is called the 'melodic minor scale'. Here are the three minor scales, using **C** as an example tonic note:

Natural Minor Scale
I	II	♭III	IV	V	♭VI	♭VII	I	(The same notes as the
C	D	E♭	F	G	A♭	B♭	C	relative E♭ major scale.)

Harmonic Minor Scale
I	II	♭III	IV	V	♭VI	VII	I
C	D	E♭	F	G	A♭	B	C

Melodic Minor Scale

Rising pitch
I	II	♭III	IV	V	VI	VII	I
C	D	E♭	F	G	A	B	C

Falling pitch
I	♭VII	♭VI	V	IV	♭III	II	I
C	B♭	A♭	G	F	E♭	D	C

Chromatic and diatonic scales

Diatonic means tone and semitone intervals. A diatonic scale means a major scale or one of its modes, i.e. the same notes in a different order. Chromatic means moving in semitones – each note is a semitone in pitch from the next. So a chromatic scale is one where all the notes are a semitone apart.

Other clefs

The alto clef covers the middle area of pitch – the lower part of the treble clef and the upper part of the bass clef. The centre of the sign indicates where middle **C** is:

THE ALTO CLEF 𝄡 MIDDLE C

The alto clef sign can be used to produce the soprano and mezzo-soprano clefs above the alto clef, and the tenor and baritone clefs below, by moving it up or down. Where the pitch of the music rises considerably, rather than use many leger lines or a change of clef, notes may be written an octave lower with '8va' above them.

Common accidentals

Particular notes are expected in each key, but there are now a number of common 'acceptable' out-of-key notes and chords, i.e. accidentals. In blues, jazz or ragtime music, certain notes are played a semitone lower than usual. These 'blue' notes are the flattened 3rd, 5th and 7th degrees of the tonic major scale, i.e. **G** natural, **B♭** and **D** natural in the key of **E** major. The chords built on these flattened notes are often used in rock music. In ragtime, major rather than minor chords built on the 2nd, 3rd and 6th degrees of the tonic scale often occur, i.e. in **G** major, a sequence like this: **G B7 E7 A7 D7** and **G**. In country and pop music, key changes for later choruses are used for variety. The key is raised by a semitone or a tone. When the tonal centre or key of the music changes temporarily (just for a note or few bars), accidentals will be used. Where the key change lasts for a whole section or till the end of the piece, a new key signature will replace the old. This example shows a change of key from **E** to **F** major:

Temporary, non-stressed chromatic notes are used in all types of music – involving a short note a semitone up or down from a scale or 'expected' note.

The circle of fifths

This diagram is often used to illustrate the relationship of different keys:

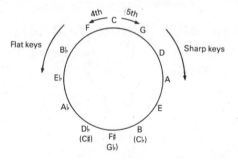

Moving round the circle clockwise, each key is a fifth higher than the previous one, i.e. **C** to **G** is a fifth up in pitch. The bottom three keys are rarely used. Chords often move up in fourths during songs – the ragtime sequence given above, for example, jumps from **G** to **B7**, then works back up through fourths to the tonic chord. A useful way of practising chords and changes is to move round the circle of fifths anticlockwise – in other words up in fourths.

APPENDIX 2 – RHYTHM

Other time signatures

The most common time signatures were examined in the rhythm section of the book. They are often categorized in three main groups – duple, triple and quadruple. Each of these groups is subdivided into simple and compound – the top number (the beat count) in compound time signatures is divisible by three. Common and uncommon time signatures are shown in their categories below:

CATEGORY	DUPLE			TRIPLE			QUADRUPLE		
Simple	2/2	2/4	2/8	3/2	3/4	3/8	4/2	4/4	4/8
Compound *(Divide beats by 3 for main stress points)*	6/4	6/8	6/16	9/4	9/8	9/16	12/4	12/8	12/16

Other more unusual time signatures can occur in music from time to time. $^5_4$ time, for example, was used for Jethro Tull's 'Living In The Past' and Dave Brubeck's 'Take Five'. This rhythm also comes into the Beatles song 'Don't Let Me Down'. Normally the five beats are split into three and two, i.e. there are stresses on the first quarter-note and the fourth. Another unusual time signature is $^7_8$ – often used in Greek music.

Occasionally the underlying stress pattern and hence the time signature changes during a piece of music. The new time is shown at the start of the bar, and the original time is indicated again when the temporary change is over. Here is an example from the Beatles song 'All You Need is Love':

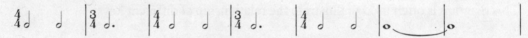

The thirty-second note (demisemiquaver)

Very occasionally you'll come across a thirty-second note. This lasts for half the length of a sixteenth-note (semiquaver). It's written with three 'flags' or 'beams':

If you find it hard to follow music with thirty-second notes in it, double the time values of all the notes and rests of the bar.

Equal notes in a beat

You've seen the triplet sign:  . This means there are three notes in the beat and they should each be equal in length. Occasionally the composer wants an unusual number of equal length notes in a beat, or over a number of beats. Then the appropriate number is placed over the notes in question:

APPENDIX 3 – INTERPRETATION

Speed

lento – very slow
largo – slow and dignified
larghetto – reasonably slow
adagio – slow
grave – slow and solemn
andante – at a moderate, 'walking' pace
moderato – moderate speed
andantino – a little faster than andante
allegretto – reasonably fast; not as fast as allegro
allegro – fast and lively
vivace – lively
presto – very fast
prestissimo – very, very fast
giusto – in exact time; at the proper speed

Volume

pianissimo (pp) – very soft
piano (p) – soft
mezzo piano (mp) – reasonably soft
mezzo forte (mf) – reasonably loud
forte (f) – loud
fortissimo (ff) – very loud

Mood

ad libitum (ad lib.) – at will; the speed and style to be determined by the performer
agitato – agitated, restlessly
affettuoso – with feeling
brillante – bright, brilliant style
cantabile ⎱
cantando ⎰ – in a singing style
con anima – with deep feeling, soulfully
con brio – with vigour
con moto – with movement
dolce – sweetly
doloroso ⎱
lacrimoso ⎬ – sorrowfully
mesto ⎰

Change of speed

allargando (allarg.) – becoming slower and broader
accelerando (accel.) – becoming faster, gradually
a tempo ⎱
tempo primo ⎰ back to the original speed after change
calando – becoming slower *and* softer
doppio movimento – double the speed
meno mosso – immediately slower
più allegro – faster
più mosso – immediately faster
rallentando (rall.) ⎱
ritardando (ritard.) ⎰ gradually becoming slower
ritenuto (rit.) held back, slightly slower
slentando – gradually slower
stringendo (string) – gradually faster

Change in volume

crescendo (cresc.) – becoming gradually louder (marked ⏝)
decrescendo (decresc.) ⎱ becoming gradually softer (marked
diminuendo (dim.) ⎰ ⏞)
forte piano (fp) – loud, then soft
morendo ⎱
smorzando ⎰ dying away
perdendosi – dying away and becoming slower
più forte – louder
più piano – softer
sforzando (sf) – a strong emphasis or accent
rinforzando (rf) – a reinforcement

espressivo (espresso.) – with expression
facile – easily
giocoso – with humour
glissando (gliss.) – sliding through adjacent notes
largamente – broadly
leggiero – lightly, delicately
maestoso – grandly, majestically
marcato – markedly, with emphasis on each note
risoluto – boldly
rubato – robbed time, ad lib flexible style
spiritoso ⎱
vivo ⎰ – lively
staccato – detached
strepitoso – noisy
vigoroso – boldly

Articulation and phrasing

slur – curved line joining two notes of different pitch. They should be played smoothly.

phrase mark – curved line round a number of notes to indicate the composer's intention for punctuation or phrasing of the music:

legato – a term meaning a group of notes should be played smoothly, one to the next.
glissando (gliss.) – a slide (up or down a string or on the keyboard the back of a finger running quickly across the white keys)
staccato – the note should be stopped short:
accent – the note should be stressed when any of those signs are used: > v ᐟ -
fermata – a note should be held longer than written: ⌢
grace note – a small note with a line through it right next to a normal note is deemed to have no time value. It should be played very quickly:

A note from the Author

My music course has furnished you with all the fundamental and necessary information to understand, read and play music. The later sections also provided arranging ideas and various avenues to explore. Now you have a strong base on which to enlarge your store of musical knowledge and ideas.

To make the most of what you've learnt, you'll need to listen, follow and analyse as much music of different kinds as possible – approach any problem or piece of music with fascination and interest rather than thinking of it as just a task to complete before you can tackle the next.

You should also try composing songs and instrumental pieces of your own, experimenting with variations in rhythm and pitch from the expected patterns and notes – this will strengthen your feel for music structure as well as be interesting and enjoyable to do.

Today's musician is expected to, and wants to, understand and play all types of music. By knowing the theory behind melodies and arrangements as well as being able to read and follow them, and by analysing variations as they come along, you will acquire the necessary versatility – and in the process enjoy music all the more!.

Russ Shipton

The companion book *Russ Shipton's Music Course – Keyboards* is also available from Pan Books Ltd.

About the author

Photograph by Jane Bown

Russ Shipton is the author of over forty music tuition books, including *The Complete Guitar Player* series, which is the best-selling guitar course in the world, with ¾ million copies sold to date. As well as writing and teaching, he has been a regular performing musician for sixteen years – developing a varied repertoire that has been passed on in his books to great effect. A self-taught musician, and therefore not 'locked-in' to the standard, classical form of tuition, Russ always takes a fresh and practical approach to each area of music he is teaching – and writes the kind of books he needed (but could never find) when he started playing.

Russ began his musical career at the age of 23, after an economics degree and several years of accountancy. By analysing the styles and techniques of other players, he improved his own playing and widened his repertoire. Since 1973 he has performed in Australia, Europe and the UK, as well as teaching both privately and in schools. Russ has also toured the world with a theatre group, ran a West End music club, and written songs for Thames TV. In 1981 he co-wrote the winning entry for the 'Song for London' competition, singing the song live in New York on NBC's *Today* programme. In 1983 he appeared on TV and radio in Australia to promote the *Complete Guitar Player* series (published by Music Sales), and in 1984 the course was published in America, including a 60-minute video completed that year. Between 1984 and 1987 Russ wrote his *Rock and Pop* books (published by IMP) plus a number of other titles.

Russ came to Pan Books in 1987 with his ideas for a 'new approach' to teaching music theory, and was commissioned to complete two companion books with a practical bias – one for guitarists, the other for keyboard players, with each to have a matching cassette including demonstrations of all the examples in the book. The result is a breakthrough in music tuition.